KU-419-154

Trust the Universe

To Alexis, Amelia, and Aidyn:
May you follow your heart and
manifest your wildest dreams.

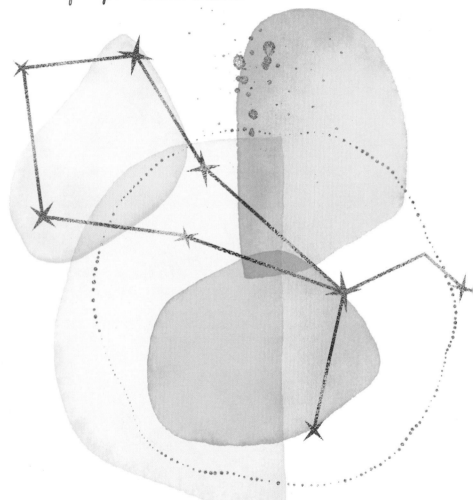

Trust the Universe

Powerful Methods for Positive Manifestation and Raising your Vibration

Stephanie Keith

ROCK POINT
QUARTOKNOWS.COM
NEW YORK, NY

CONT

ENTS

Dear Universe,
Thank you for leading
me on this path toward
joy, fulfillment, and
possibility.

INTRODUCTION

··

When I put the key in the front door of my dream home and stepped through the door, it was like stepping into a new reality. A reality I created. A reality that just three months prior didn't seem possible, that everyone told me was unreasonable and far-fetched.

It was confirmation for me that when you trust the Universe, you can co-create your reality. We all have this infinite power within us. If we become aware and intentional, anything is possible.

I vowed to make it my mission to share this with the world and teach others how to access this power and manifest their dreams.

Months earlier, I was sitting in my little, nearly hundred-year-old home staring at the leaky window as it rained, feeling helpless because I knew I didn't have the money to repair it. As I held my newborn daughter, a flood of anxiety washed over me as I began thinking about my old home and all the dangers that possibly lurked beyond the walls, like black mold, lead paint, and old electrical wiring. As I looked down at this sweet, innocent baby who was dependent on me for everything, I knew I wanted to give her the best life possible, but I had no idea how I would make it happen.

My husband was laid off from his job, and with no college degree combined with living in a rural area, job prospects were slim. I was in an entry-level job barely making enough to pay the bills. Every last cent of my paycheck went to paying for diapers and formula. I was living six hours away from my family, feeling lost, stuck, and hopeless.

Then something incredible happened. My mom mailed me a book and told me I had to read it. I will never forget the feeling of holding this book in my hand and reading a quote on the first page from the *Emerald Tablet* that said "As above, so below. As within, so without." I felt every atom of my being light up with excitement. It was as if I were reunited with an old friend, an ancient piece of wisdom I had long forgotten about. While I couldn't explain it, I had the knowledge deep in my heart that this book would change my life.

The Law of Attraction requires your unwavering belief to work, so allow yourself to believe in all possibilities and fully embody the practices in this book.

Little did I know that within three months, my life would be completely transformed. Every area of my life that was lacking completely turned around! I manifested the exact amount of money I needed for a down payment on my dream home. I received a promotion that doubled my salary. My husband was then able to go back to college to pursue his career goals, and my mom moved close by to help take care of my daughter while I worked. The circumstances that led to these incredible changes were nothing short of miraculous.

Once I realized the power within me, I set the intention to manifest a life I didn't need a vacation from. A life where I would truly feel alive waking up every morning with joy, gratitude, and excitement. A life where I experienced true freedom and could do what I love and desire every day. A life filled with passion and meaning.

I have since manifested a multipassion business, financial freedom, and more joy and fulfillment than I could have ever imagined. My intention for you is that you use the tools within this book to manifest a life you don't need a vacation from. Allow this book to assist you in stepping into your higher power and achieving fulfillment, joy, and more love than you ever thought possible.

My wish for you is to manifest:

* A life where you become massively abundant doing what you love.
* A life where every day is filled with love and joy.
* A life that knows no limits.
* A life that you create based on your desires.

While reading this book, I ask that you suspend all skepticism and disbelief. Think of it as a science experiment where you are testing out the practices in this book. The thing to remember is that in order to manifest your desires, you must fully believe in the possibility of them happening and drop the doubt and skepticism. What do you have to lose by trying? Worst-case scenario, nothing happens and you're no worse off than you are now. Best-case scenario, you manifest a life beyond your wildest dreams. Isn't it worth giving it a try? Keep an open mind and let the magic unfold. Are you ready to step into the realm of infinite possibilities? You're only one decision away from the life of your dreams.

My energy creates my reality. I am ready and willing to use this power with intention and for good.

THE LAW
OF
ATTRACTION

It all starts with understanding energy and frequency and how they construct life as we know it. Take a look around you. Everything that you see started out as a thought. Your home, your car, your clothes, your phone, and this book all originated as a thought in someone's mind. Someone had an inspired idea and used their imagination to visualize it. They believed in the possibility of it and planned out the details in their mind before it ever became a physical reality. Everything starts in the mind. It is from there that all reality is created. Your thoughts create things and what you focus on expands: this is known as the Law of Attraction.

The Law of Attraction states that you can manifest anything if you ask the Universe for what you want, have unwavering faith it will be delivered, and are open to receiving it by taking inspired action.

Everything is energy. If you look at anything with a strong enough microscope, you'll find that nothing is solid. Everything is made up of tiny particles vibrating at different frequencies. The chair you're sitting on, the book you're holding, and even your body is not truly solid—they too are energy that is constantly in motion.

All energy is interconnected, both here on planet Earth and in the Universe. What does this mean? It means you are one with the Universe. You are more powerful than you know! One rule is constant: the energy you put out is the energy you receive back. What shows up in your physical reality is a direct reflection of the energy you are giving off through your thoughts, feelings, and vibration.

The Law of Attraction works in tandem with other universal laws like the Law of Vibration. In order to impress your thoughts onto the electromagnetic field around you, feelings must be associated with the thoughts. Feelings amplify thoughts. Think of it like a volume button. The stronger you feel, the louder the message is to the Universe. The feelings that are consistent determine your vibrational frequency. You can match your vibrational frequency with that of your desired reality.

While the Law of Attraction hasn't become a popular term until recently, it has been working since the dawn of time. There are hints of it throughout many religious texts, but the masses haven't become aware of it or taught about it until around the last century or so. It is thought that those in power kept this knowledge inside their inner circles to retain their power over the people, but not anymore. It's time for everyone to become aware of this wisdom and start creating the life of their dreams.

The three basic steps of the Law of Attraction that are most commonly taught are asking the Universe for what you want, fully believing it will be delivered, and opening yourself to receiving it. While these steps lay the basic framework, a lot of things can get in the way. Throughout the book, we will dive deep into practices that will help you overcome the barriers to manifesting.

Just like the Law of Gravity, the Law of Attraction is always working, whether you are aware of it or not. It has been working your entire life to attract things into your reality even when you didn't know this law existed. Think about babies that are learning to walk. They don't understand the Law of Gravity, yet they will still inevitably fall and hit the ground as they learn how to take those first steps. The Law of Gravity doesn't care that they are just babies and don't yet understand the law. It doesn't show favoritism nor discrimination. It is always working for everyone all the time. It is the same with the Law of Attraction. You have always been attracting things into your reality. You just haven't been aware of it, so you have been creating your reality on autopilot. Imagine how much your life would change if you began intentionally creating your reality.

What Is Reality?

Quantum physics and what's known as "the observer effect" tell us that there are multiple wavelengths or probabilities that exist. The probability that turns into reality is the one that is expected based on the observer—you. Your brain uses your past experiences, beliefs, thoughts, and vibration with your five senses to collapse these wavelengths into your reality. This is why even though everything is moving energy, our brain processes things as solid. It is nothing more than your perception of the world around you based on your thoughts, beliefs, and experiences combined with your five senses. What this means is that nothing truly exists in form until you observe it. In theory, if you walk out of the room you're in, it doesn't exist as solid matter. It's when you enter the room and observe it that your expectations actually create the solid matter you see before you. Reality doesn't seem too real after all, does it?

Those same thoughts, beliefs, and experiences that create your reality can also be used to alter your reality. You have the power to change your thoughts, feelings, and vibration; therefore, you have the power to change your reality regardless of your past, where you were born, how old you are, and what your current life circumstances are.

Being, Not Doing

A common misconception with the Law of Attraction is that you can visualize what you want or write it down in a journal, do a few affirmations, and it will simply fall into your lap immediately. The Law of Attraction isn't about *doing*. It's about *being*. You can't do affirmations in the morning, then go back to being negative the rest of the day and expect your desire to manifest. The Law of Attraction responds to your energy—the energy you hold most often. It doesn't matter what ritual you try if you aren't dedicated to stepping into this new version of yourself where you focus more on what you want than what you don't want.

This is why lottery winners almost always end up losing all of their money. They won the lottery, yet their beliefs and attitudes haven't changed. They continue living with a lack mindset; therefore, lack continues showing up for them.

Think about how you've been showing up in life. Do you generally look at the bright side of things or are you always complaining? Are you kind and generous to others or do you think everyone is out to get you? Are you excited about the future or always worrying about it? These questions can give you clues as to why certain scenarios keep playing out in your life.

If you do lean more toward the negative side, not to worry. It's never too late to make a change. The tools throughout this book will help you get there if you want to and believe you can.

I am ready to begin
my journey of
manifesting miracles
in my life. I am willing
to keep an open
mind and trust the
Universe.

Believing in the Possible

In order to manifest what you desire; you must believe it is possible. When I first read the book that introduced me to the Law of Attraction, I decided to go all in and fully believe in any and all possibilities. I let my imagination go wild. I opened myself up to the possibility of magic and miracles. I suspended all skepticism and doubt. I viewed it as a game because, why not? What did I have to lose? With that mindset, I began experiencing life in a way I never thought possible.

The same can be true for you. I am asking you to keep an open mind as you go through this book. Consider this—at one point in time, if you were to tell people they could light up a room with the flip of a switch without the use of candles, they would've thought you were talking about magic and said it's not possible.

A few decades ago, if you tried to explain what a smartphone or WiFi was, people would have said they were science fiction and not possible. Now, everyone uses these technologies and they have become standard parts of our everyday life.

I believe the same is true for the Law of Attraction, and it will be used and accepted by everyone to create a better world free of unnecessary pain and suffering.

You have the gift of free will. No one else is responsible for creating your reality. You alone control your thoughts, feelings, and vibration. It is within you, not any external person or circumstance. You are in the driver's seat. Are you ready to take your life off autopilot and start truly living a life of fulfillment?

Focus on what you want instead of what you don't want. Instead of focusing on getting out of debt, focus on creating abundance.

I manifest my dreams effortlessly.

CHAPTER

2

WHAT IS MANIFESTATION?

Manifesting is the act of your desires showing up in your physical reality. It is the action taken to bring the principles of the Law of Attraction into your life.

You are connected to an infinite source of energy and wisdom. Throughout this book, I will refer to this as the Universe, but feel free to use whatever word has meaning for you—God, Source, Higher Power, etc. You are always connected to this energy; therefore, you are always communicating with the Universe through your thoughts, feelings, and vibration. Your thoughts trigger feelings and when you feel something deep enough and long enough, it can shift your energetic vibration, aligning you with the vibrational frequency of your desired reality.

Just as you can tune into different radio stations, you can tune into different vibrational frequencies. The more feeling you give to your thoughts and the longer you sit in those thoughts and feelings, the stronger the signal is to the Universe.

Luckily, there is a delay. This is good, because if the things we thought and felt manifested instantly, we'd be in big trouble. That would mean every bad, scary, or hateful thought we had would come to fruition! Imagine paying your bills and feeling overwhelmed with debt. If the Universe manifested instantly, you would find yourself in a mountain of debt! Thankfully, the Universe responds to what you think and feel the majority of the time. This dictates your energetic vibration. If you think and feel positive thoughts and emotions more than fifty percent of the time, you will tip the scales toward a high vibration, and manifest more high-vibrational things. If you feel negative most of the time, you will attract more negative circumstances into your life.

Have you ever met people who are always seeing the glass as half empty? They could win the lottery, but instead of feeling grateful, they'd just complain about how much the government will take in taxes. These people are negative the majority of the time and living in a lower vibration.

Likewise, you probably also know people who are always optimistic. They're always smiling and things always seem to work out for them. These people are positive the majority of the time and living in a higher vibration.

Most of us are somewhere in the middle. Which is why it's so important to become aware of your thoughts, feelings, and vibration, and continue to focus on people, places, and experiences that raise your vibration.

How to Manifest

Your feelings are your inner guidance system. Think of them as feedback from the Universe. They are letting you know whether or not you are on the right track. When in doubt, focus on what feels good and you will shift your vibration.

There are two types of manifesting: manifesting from the ego and manifesting from the higher self.

Universe,
I am ready to see things
in a new light.
I trust you will guide me
down the right path,
and I am ready
and willing to open myself
to new possibilities.
I cast away any
doubt and surrender to
you completely.

Manifesting From Your Ego

When you are manifesting from your ego, you are manifesting what you *think* will make you happy. Oftentimes, this is something that looks great on the outside, but lacks substance and isn't what will make you make you happy in the long run. This also may be what our brain tells us is reasonable.

The ego is logical and practical. It uses stored beliefs and experiences to shape your decisions. The ego is there to protect you. It's like the parents who push you down one path because they want what is best for you, even though that particular path may not be what makes you happy. That path may logically seem like the safest choice, but if it doesn't give you fulfillment, is it really the right path? I don't believe so. There is a better way, an easier way, and it involves tapping into your higher self.

Our brain can process up to four hundred billion bits of information per second. Even though that is an extraordinary number, it is still only a fraction of what surrounds us in any given moment. As human beings, we are only capable of being consciously aware of around two thousand bits per second. That leaves a lot of information out of our conscious awareness. This is why we are limited when only using the ego to manifest. We have our blinders on and can only understand the path that is a part of our conscious awareness. This is where our higher self can step in and help us manifest our desires in the best possible way that will lead to fulfillment.

Hold the vibration of love as often as possible.

It is our natural state and the highest vibrational frequency.

manifesting from Your Higher Self

When you are manifesting from your higher self, you are manifesting what will truly make you happy.

When I first learned of the Law of Attraction, I made manifesting money my top priority. I felt like that would make all my problems go away and leave me feeling happy and fulfilled. That couldn't have been further from the truth. I was too focused on *how* I would manifest money instead of trusting the Universe to deliver my desires in the best, most fulfilling way. I thought I needed to be practical.

The problem was the only "practical" means of manifesting money that was in my awareness at the time was through my corporate job. I was so focused on the way I would manifest money that I didn't give the Universe any other options to work with.

I began manifesting all sorts of money through raises, bonuses, and promotions. With every raise, more responsibility was placed on my shoulders, and I found myself more and more stressed and miserable.

It got to the point where I had no life outside of work. I would leave for work early while it was dark outside, and by the time I got home, I had just enough time to make my daughter dinner and give her a bath before her bedtime.

I was missing out on my daughter's milestones, fighting with my husband, completely neglecting self-care, and feeling anxious during every waking moment. I lived for the weekends and my two weeks of vacation every year. I spent all day Sunday dreading Monday. But I kept pushing through because I told myself the money would give my daughter the best life possible.

It all came to a breaking point on my thirtieth birthday. As I reflected on my twenties, I came to the realization that I had given an entire decade to a

job that filled me with dread and anxiety. I knew I couldn't continue down this path another ten years, or thirty for that matter. I realized the money wasn't worth it if it was keeping me from enjoying life with the ones I loved most.

It was in that low moment of wallowing that I connected with my higher self. All of a sudden, I felt a sense of calm assurance wash over me. A voice inside of me said, "Freedom. It's not the money. It's the freedom you thought money would give you that you're truly after. You want to manifest a life you don't need a vacation from."

I didn't want to wait until retirement to start truly living and enjoying all life has to offer. I wanted every day to feel like a vacation. I wanted to wake up feeling excited instead of filled with dread. I wanted to go to the beach in the middle of the week. I wanted to attend all of my daughter's school functions.

In that moment, it all became so clear to me that by worrying about *how* I would manifest money, I was limiting myself from the infinite possibilities that surrounded me. In that moment of realization, I fully surrendered and trusted the Universe to deliver.

Shortly after, I had the idea for the Law of Attraction Tribe Instagram page, which turned into a business giving me a platform to teach people all over the globe about the Law of Attraction through books, courses, and a podcast. The Universe paved the perfect path toward fulfillment, happiness, and abundance.

Your higher self knows no limits. It is connected to the infinite wisdom of the Universe and can see far beyond what the human brain can process. It will lead you down the path of least resistance toward true joy and fulfillment. Trust it and embrace it.

I am divinely guided toward my destiny.

THE
HIGHER SELF

As we dive into manifesting, we'll explore the ego versus your higher self a little more deeply.

In our society, we are programmed to make decisions from the ego. It is the voice of logic and reason, and its sole job is to keep us safe, often leaving no room for spirituality or imagination. It works very hard to avoid fearful situations based on past experiences and beliefs.

Your higher self is always tapped into the infinite power and wisdom of the Universe. It is a clear channel of communication between source energy and you. It sees the big picture and understands the magnificence of what's in store for you. The higher self is calm, collected, and certain. It is the real you.

Your higher self doesn't always seem logical at first. It gives you bits of information piece by piece and requires trust that it will guide you down the right path.

Your higher self lives in the now. Where the ego believes that you need something first before you will feel happy and fulfilled, the higher self understands that you have the ability to be happy now. Being in a state of love, gratitude, and joy now will align you with the manifestation that will bring you even more joy and fulfillment.

When manifesting with the ego, it will never be enough. If you are continually looking outside of yourself for happiness, it will elude you. It's fleeting. You may manifest what you think you want, but you will always have the feeling of needing more to sustain happiness.

By connecting with your higher self, you develop the understanding that happiness comes from within. You have access to it anytime, regardless of external circumstances.

Follow Your Inner Guide

You can use your feelings as a gauge for whether you are manifesting with your ego or higher self. Remember, your feelings serve as an inner guidance system. Feeling good now is an indicator of being connected with your higher self. Thinking you will feel good once some external factor manifests is an indicator you are operating from the ego.

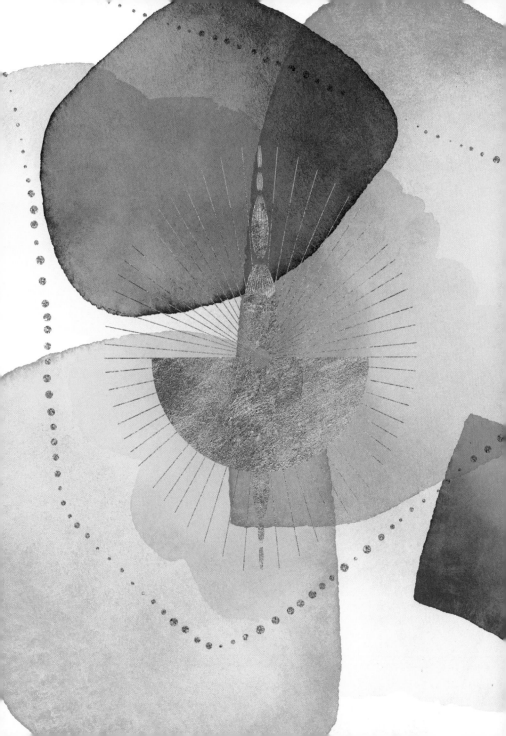

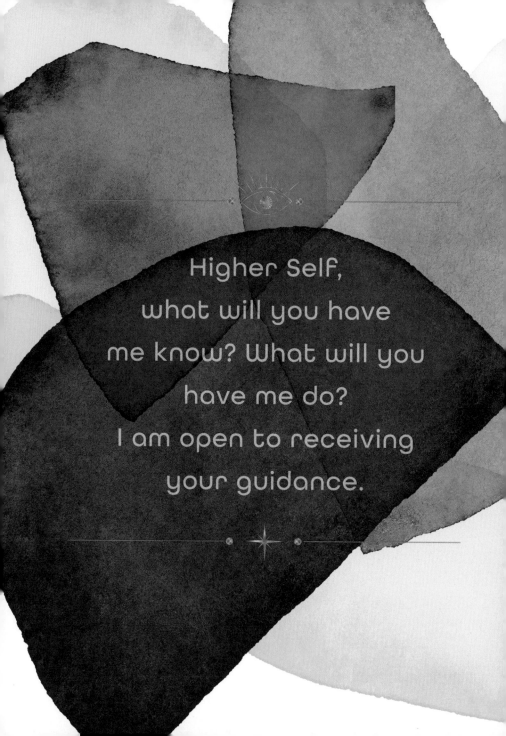

Higher Self,
what will you have
me know? What will you
have me do?
I am open to receiving
your guidance.

Another sign you are connected with your higher self is operating from a place of ease versus resistance. Our society teaches us that hard work yields results. But as I explained earlier, this is coming from the limited thinking of a brain that remains practical. Imagine swimming against the current of a river. It's not natural and doesn't feel good. It feels forced. There is an easier way. When you finally let go, you simply flow with the natural current. Surrender and let your higher self guide you down the path of least resistance.

Think about the times when you manifested from the ego. You took the logical or reasonable path in making a decision. How did this feel? What was the outcome?

I manifested from my ego for years. I stayed at my corporate job even though I was miserable and it impacted my life in negative ways. I stayed for the money because that was the normal and practical thing to do. I stayed because I was worried what others would think if I quit a secure, good-paying job. I stayed because I was fearful and doubtful that I could make a good income doing what I love. This led to a lot of unnecessary suffering and eventually burnout, where I began having panic attacks at work. I knew it didn't feel good staying, but I let fear take over and keep me stuck in a negative situation for far too long.

Recognize Your Higher Self

Your higher self fully understands your oneness with the Universe. It knows that your manifestation has already happened. In fact, quantum physics tells us there are an infinite number of realities. We just have to align with the frequency of the reality we want. Where the ego only knows one way to get there, the higher self is able to align you with the path of greatest fulfillment. It is in a space of knowing it is already done. You just need to energetically align with it.

When you are manifesting from your higher self, you will have unwavering faith your desires will manifest in the best possible way. We often try to control how things happen, but this is not needed. Your higher self always knows the best way to get you from point A to point B.

Almost every incredible thing I've manifested didn't happen the way I would have imagined. When I haven't been able to manifest or it took much longer than expected, it was because I was trying to control how it would happen instead of trusting the Universe to deliver it to me in the best possible way.

When you begin stepping into your higher self, you feel inspired to take action. It doesn't feel like hard work or a chore you have to get done. It excites you and energizes you.

This is divine manifesting. You don't have to settle for mediocre. You can create a life that fulfills you in all areas. No sacrifices need to be made. We often think in order to achieve greatness, we have to give something up in return. But this is not true. You don't have to hold on to things that are not serving your highest good. You can let go of anything that feels hard or forced. With divine manifesting, you can manifest your desires in a way that feels easy and fun.

Trust the Divine

Think about a time when you manifested from your higher self. You took inspired action even though it may not have made sense and people around you didn't understand it. How did it feel? What was the outcome?

One of my boldest manifestations that came from my higher self was when I moved to Florida. I knew ever since I was eight years old that someday I would move to Florida and buy a house with a pool. It was a place where I felt alive, where stress seemed to melt away, the sun was always shining, and people seemed happier. There were many times I thought about moving there but let fear and uncertainty get in the way.

In 2015, we were at a crossroads where my husband was finishing college and looking for a job, and my daughter was getting ready to enter kindergarten. I knew that once she was in school and he got settled in a job, it would be harder to move, as there would be too many things holding us down. I knew this was the time to make the move. I felt more certain than ever.

I talked to my husband about it, expecting him to be against it as he had been many times before. This time, though, there was no arguing or pushback. To my surprise, he simply agreed.

We set a date for when we wanted to move. I put in my notice at work before having another job lined up and fully trusted the process, taking inspired action one step at a time.

Make gratitude a daily practice to stay connected with your higher self.

Give gratitude for what you already have and gratitude for what you desire as though it's already yours.

Even though we were moving to a city we had never visited, where we knew no one and had no jobs lined up, I felt absolutely certain this was the right decision.

My coworkers, boss, and friends all tried to talk me out of it. They couldn't believe I was moving with no set plan or job lined up. They kept trying to place doubt in my mind, but my higher self stepped in with assurance and inspired action.

Just as we were nearing our moving date, a friend of mine within my company got a promotion, putting him in charge of the state of Florida! I knew this was no coincidence. I immediately called him and explained my situation. Within two weeks, he called me and told me to hop on a plane because I had an interview lined up in Tampa.

My husband and I flew down for the interview and to look for a place to rent. My interview went great, and I was offered the position on the spot. After we secured a rental, my husband felt inspired to walk into the hospital and see if there was an opening in the respiratory department. He happened to run into the head of the department, who also had just moved from out of state and was renting in the same complex we were! Talk about divine timing and taking inspired action! They hit it off and he was given an interview and landed the job.

The higher self knows that where there is a will, there is a way. It does not worry that a job isn't lined up or all the answers haven't yet appeared, because it understands that we operate in a Universe of infinite possibilities, and you can manifest anything you need or want.

Had I been operating from my ego, I would have come up with endless excuses for why this wouldn't work. I would have listened to everyone who told me this move was crazy. Instead, I trusted the Universe to deliver and it did not let me down. I stepped into my higher self and remained empowered to fulfill my desire.

Learn to Listen to Your Higher Self

You are always connected to your higher self, but you may not be aware of it; therefore, you're tuning it out. Think about listening to music. When you are quiet and tuned into the music, you feel it. You hear the lyrics. You dance along to it. You truly experience the song. Now imagine the same song is playing, but you are talking on the phone. Now you're not tuned into it. It's there and it's playing, but you aren't listening to the lyrics or moving to the rhythm. You may even be completely oblivious to it. This is how it is for most of us when we are not yet aware of our higher self. But as you become aware, and learn how to tune in, you will create a clear channel and a deeper understanding of the greater power you have unlimited access to.

Learning how to connect with your higher self takes some practice at first. But just like anything, the more you do it, the more it becomes second nature. Eventually, you will be able to quickly access your higher self.

Remember your feelings are your inner guidance system. Tap into good feelings like love, joy, and gratitude and you will tap into your higher power. If you are feeling negative, it's time to clear your mind and reconnect.

MEDITATION
FOR CONNECTING WITH YOUR HIGHER SELF

First, create a sacred, relaxing environment where you feel safe and can easily calm your mind.

Find a quiet space where you can sit uninterrupted. This can even be outside where you are surrounded by nature and fresh air. You may choose to cleanse the energy of the space with sage or Florida water. Bring in things that help you relax, like candles, incense, or crystals.

Next, sit down cross-legged or in a chair. If sitting on the ground, you can prop a pillow underneath you. Keep your back, neck, and head straight so you are a straight channel for energy to flow through you.

When you are comfortable, close your eyes and bring your attention to the breath without trying to control it.

Now imagine a golden light coming down from the Universe through your Sahasrara or crown chakra (top of the head) and traveling down your spine right into the earth. This loving and healing light is going through you and wrapping around the earth's core and flowing back up through you and back to the Source. This beautiful, pure light fills your entire being with every breath, and with each exhale, you release anything that is no longer serving you. You are now safely rooted and a clear channel for connecting with your higher self.

As you bask in this golden light, you can call on the Universe to connect you with your higher self. Place your hands on your heart and feel this light radiate from your heart and surround you. You have established your connection with the Source and can now receive guidance from your higher self.

The answers
I need are already
within me.

EMBRACING YOUR POWER

It's time to set aside the notion that you are a victim of circumstance and embrace the power that lies within you. You are in control of your life story. You get to write the next chapter. It's time to use this power and consciously co-create with the Universe.

One of the things that successful manifesters do is make a decision about what they want. They don't wish for it; they decide it will happen and don't let anything stand in the way. Instead of making excuses, they hold the vision. While most people wait for external circumstances to perfectly align, successful manifesters know they have everything they need already within them.

As you continue to expand your awareness and embrace your power, you will continue to energetically grow, taking you from lack to abundance. In order to continue manifesting more, you must focus on abundance and believe it exists. Contrary to what we've been taught, abundance is our natural state. Just look at nature. Everything is perfectly created for abundance. Every seed can grow an entire plant.

Be Aware of Abundance

A great way to expand your awareness of the vast abundance that surrounds us is to look to the cosmos. Our universe is so vast and expansive, it's hard for our human brains to truly comprehend. The observable universe is almost twenty-eight-billion light years in diameter. To put this into perspective, one light year is over five trillion miles. This is only what can be observed. Beyond that, it could be infinite, and we know that it is always expanding.

Despite the vast abundance that surrounds us, society has programmed us to be okay with having just enough. You don't have to settle for just getting by or having a little extra. As nature and the universe demonstrate, there is always more than enough. There is no lack. The only lack that exists is the lack our human minds have created. It is nothing more than a human construct and only exists because we are not aware of the abundance that surrounds us.

Expand Your Consciousness

Just as the universe is continually expanding, you can expand your consciousness. You can expand your awareness, and you can expand the abundance you experience in all areas of your life.

Quantum theorists believe there are an infinite number of parallel realities. In order to create the reality you want, you must energetically align with it. You do this by acting, thinking, and feeling as though it is already yours *now*.

* ✳ How would you show up if all your dreams came true?
* ✳ What would you think?
* ✳ How would you feel?

The key is to tap into those feelings now. Tap into that confidence and self-worth now.

Subconscious Obstacles

Most people try to manifest by changing their environment. This is why so many diets fail and people quit going to the gym one or two months after getting a gym membership. They aren't sticking with it because they haven't changed their subconscious beliefs that say they are overweight or unhealthy.

Your subconscious gets in the way by telling you all of the reasons why this can't happen, why you don't deserve it, and why it's unrealistic, leaving you full of doubt. This is disempowering and doesn't serve you.

Here's why it happens. During the first seven years of life, you are in the theta brain wave state. This is what I refer to as a hypnotic state. You absorb everything around you. It's like you are a computer and in the first seven years of life, you are downloading all of your software programs. You are downloading this information from your parents, family, teachers, friends, and anyone else you come into contact with regularly, as well as the media.

Some of these programs are essential. They teach you how to function in society, follow the rules, abide by cultural norms, and stay safe. However, you also pick up on negative and fear-based beliefs. These programs stay with you for the rest of your life, and society tends to continually reinforce them. Your subconscious will continue to look for evidence of these beliefs in your environment.

When I was in seventh grade, I had a history teacher who had an overall pessimistic attitude about life. Nearly every day, she would tell us, "Life is hard, folks. Get used to it." This echoed what my dad always said about how making money was hard. As I got older and faced challenges in life, I would just accept it and tell myself that it was normal because life was hard. It limited me from seeing better situations around me because my subconscious firmly believed that no matter what, life was going to be hard. My subconscious searched for evidence that aligned with this belief until I learned how to disprove it and reprogram my subconscious.

The subconscious is the dominant part of the mind. You may think you are consciously in control of your life, but the truth is your subconscious is in control ninety-nine percent of the time. You may consciously want something, but if it contradicts your subconscious beliefs,

Always talk about your desires in the past tense as though you already manifested them.

it will probably not manifest. The subconscious works very hard to maintain the status quo. It follows your beliefs and values and believes they are absolute truths, so if anything contradicts them, your subconscious doesn't trust them and works very hard at protecting you from them.

Reprogram Your Subconscious

Luckily, there is a way to reprogram the beliefs that are not serving your highest good. After age seven, the subconscious only learns through repetition. This is how you can update that old software program with new, abundant beliefs.

"I am" affirmations are my favorite way to reprogram the beliefs that are not serving your highest good. The subconscious can't distinguish between reality and imagination, so by speaking, acting, and thinking as though you've already achieved your desires, the subconscious will think this is reality and stop resisting it.

When I was still in my corporate job dealing with anxiety and feeling powerless, I began using "I am" affirmations to tell a new story and shape the reality I wanted to create. I imagined what I wanted my ideal day to look like and used that to form my affirmations. Every day, first thing in the morning, I would repeat, "I am my own boss. I make my own schedule. I am a successful author and entrepreneur. I am living my purpose. I am fulfilled in my work." These affirmations helped me embrace my power and step into this new version of my life by acting as if it had already happened and embodying the feelings of it already happening. I would repeat the affirmations over and over again until I felt gratitude and joy, as though this was already my reality.

You can put this into practice by using the words "I am" followed by whatever your new, empowering belief is. Here are some examples, but feel free to play with this and use words that leave you feeling empowered:

    ✳ I am abundant.
    ✳ I am worthy of all I desire.
    ✳ I am the creator of my life.

Using the words "I am" puts you in the present moment of already having what you desire now. It puts you in the state of embodying it and already living it. This, combined with the feelings of having it now, is what will make you an energetic magnet for what you desire.

The key is repetition. This is how the subconscious learns. Affirmations are especially powerful right before you fall asleep, when your brain is back in the theta state. Reading, writing, or listening to an affirmation recording before bed will help reprogram your subconscious quickly. You can also set reminders in your phone, put sticky notes on your bathroom mirror, or do anything else that will remind you to continue this process of repetition.

Over time, your new empowering beliefs will become dominant and quiet the doubt and fear-based beliefs. Your subconscious will accept these new beliefs as familiar and stop resisting them. It will also begin to look for evidence in your environment that supports these new beliefs.

MEDITATION
FOR EMBRACING YOUR POWER

I am one with the abundant Universe, and I choose to step into my natural state of abundance. I am a clear channel to co-create my desires with the Universe. I am worthy and deserving of all that I desire. I am invoking this powerful energy and stepping into my higher power to consciously create my reality.

I am healthy, happy, and whole.

• • •

I am safe and loved.

• • •

I am one with the Universe.

I hold the wisdom of the Universe inside of me.

INTUITION

Ever since I was a little girl, my parents taught me to listen to my intuition. My mom referred to it as my gut instinct. Whenever I had an important decision to make, she would ask me what my gut was telling me. Even my dad, who is very practical and not spiritual at all, believes we have a sixth sense. He would explain to me that the human brain can only process so much, so we need to rely on our sixth sense to help us. If something feels off, it is, so always trust your intuition. Even if you're worried it will make you seem silly, it's better to be safe than sorry.

I remember when I was in my final year of college dealing with major anxiety and stress. I felt like I was falling apart and all I wanted to do was run away from my problems. I sat in the kitchen with my mom and asked her if I should just quit. Instead of giving me a lecture about how I was ruining my life, she calmly told me to get out of my head, quit worrying about what everyone else thought, and listen to what my gut was telling me. She asked me to visualize myself ten years from now looking back on this moment and feel what I would be feeling then. Once again, she asked, "What is your gut saying to you?" In that moment, I knew with absolute certainty I should finish out the year and graduate. It wasn't what I wanted to hear, but I knew it was for my highest good.

Imagine if every life-altering decision could be made so easily. What if the answer was clearly given to us, and all we had to do was ask? The good news is, the answer *is* always there! You just need to ask. Your intuition is at your disposal whenever you need it to guide you anytime you feel lost, doubtful, or afraid. It will always lead you down the path for your highest good.

I have learned to listen to it and trust it, and it has never led me astray. It has kept me safe by warning me of situations and people who felt off, and it has helped steer me down the path toward a joyful, fulfilling life.

Imagine you are driving on a country road at night without a streetlight in sight. Without headlights, you wouldn't be able to see where you are going. It would be next to impossible to reach your desired destination. Even with the regular headlights on, it can be hard to see far in front of you. In this case, you need to use your bright lights. Your intuition is like those bright lights. It can see the big picture that our human senses can't possibly process. You don't need to use it all the time, but it can definitely help you get to your desired destination without any accidents or unnecessary struggle.

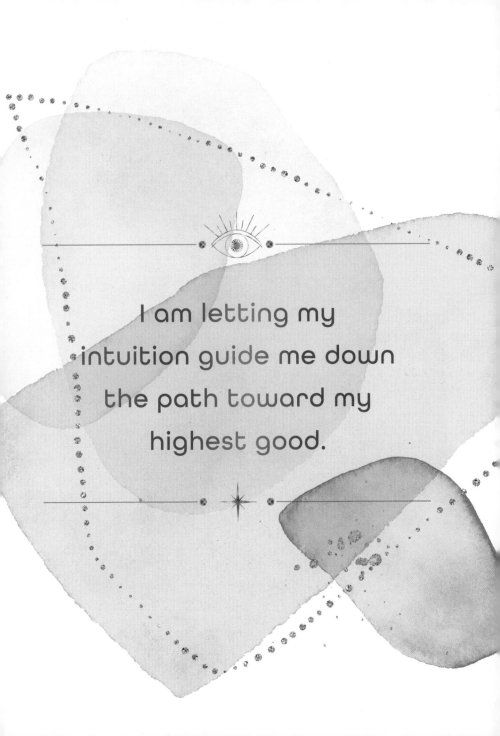

I am letting my intuition guide me down the path toward my highest good.

We all have those pivotal moments in life where one decision can take you on a completely different path. One path seems like the logical next step, yet something deep inside of you is pulling you toward a completely different path. This is your intuition steering you. Once again, it is using the bright lights to shine a light on the path your human senses may be oblivious to.

Intuition vs. Ego

Your intuition is your inner knowing. You can't explain it and it may not seem logical, but you have a strong feeling about something. Something excites you and lights you up even if it seems absurd to other people.

Doubt and limiting beliefs are the opposite. You feel uncertain. The ego will try to find the logic. If you find yourself questioning your intuition, know that this is your ego working really hard to keep the status quo. It is using your past experiences to create a possible scenario. The intuition can see far past your limited experience. It sees all possibilities and will guide you toward the best possible outcome.

Your intuition will also keep you safe and alert you if you are in a bad situation. You may be wondering how this is different from the ego. The ego will show up as panicky or anxious and may leave you with uncertainty. Just as the higher self is calm, collected, and certain, so is the intuition. You will have a deep inner knowing that something is off, where the ego will leave you feeling anxious and uncertain.

When I worked in sales for a beverage company, a lot of my business was with new bars and restaurants. One day, I received a message that a new bar was opening, and I needed to bring the paperwork to the owner to set up the account. I showed up at the bar in the middle of the day. The owner greeted me at the door and invited me inside. Instantly a very strong, unsettling feeling washed over me. I looked around the bar realizing that no one else was there. I was completely alone with this man. Just as I realized this, the man locked the door behind me and put the key in his pocket. My intuition very calmly yet firmly said *Something is up. Remain calm. Smile and say you left the paperwork in your car and need to grab it.* I told this to the owner, and he hesitated for a split second, but then unlocked the door and let me out. I walked quickly to my car, locked the doors, and sped out of there. I have no way of ever knowing what would have happened if I had ignored my intuition and stayed, but my intuition told me I was in danger.

If I were tapped into the ego at that moment, I probably would've panicked. I don't know that I would've been able to calmly come up with an excuse to be let out of the building. The ego would probably also say that there was no logical reason to fear this man. By all appearances, he seemed nonthreatening. The ego would also seem uncertain and worry what this man would think if I ran out of there. What would my company think? Would I get in trouble for bailing on a customer? What if this guy was harmless and I just lost a good account? See the difference? The ego is all over the place. It's anxious and goes back and forth second-guessing the situation trying to weigh the logical pros and cons. The intuition is absolutely certain and decisive about what needs to be done and remains calm and focused on providing the best possible path out of the bad situation. It leaves no room for questions or doubt.

To see how your intuition communicates with you, ask a question and ask for the answer within twenty-four hours. Pay attention! Your intuition can communicate subtly.

Third Eye Awakening

If you find yourself questioning whether a thought or feeling is your intuition or just self-doubt, you need to become acquainted with your intuition.

If you feel like you tend to overthink things or if you had trouble connecting with your higher self in Chapter Three, it may be because your third eye is closed.

The third eye is the gateway to heightened intuition. It is located just above and between the eyes. It's also known as the pineal gland, where the mind, body, and soul meet. It gathers information far beyond what your conscious mind can process. We are all interconnected as part of the collective consciousness. When you get a sense or feeling about something yet can't fully explain why, this is your intuition tapping into this knowledge from the collective consciousness. Manifestation requires all parts of consciousness, which is why it's important to connect with your intuition and trust it to guide you throughout life. Research has shown that meditation with a focus on the third eye region activates the pineal gland, thus awakening your third eye and heightening your intuition.

MEDITATION
TO OPEN YOUR THIRD EYE

This meditation will allow you to open your third eye and connect with your intuition.

Sit down and start taking a few deep breaths. Allow yourself to relax into the breath. If you feel anxious at all, keep focusing on the breath until you are in a state of relaxation.

Once you feel relaxed, bring your attention to the third eye region, up and between your eyes. Imagine a beautiful golden light entering through your third eye. This is the gateway to your intuition. Visualize yourself stepping through this gateway into your desired reality. Whenever you feel closed off from your intuition or second guessing it, you can do this meditation to reconnect.

• • •

CONNECTING
TO YOUR INTUITION THROUGH JOURNALING

Another method for connecting with your intuition is to ask for guidance. Get out a journal when you are feeling relaxed. You may want to do the meditation before journaling. In the journal, write, "Universe [Source, God—whatever feels good to you], guide me on the path to my highest good. What do I need to know? What do I need to do?" Allow the words to flow without judgment. When you are done writing, go back and read it. Take inspired action on whatever comes through.

I intentionally create my reality.

6

INTENTION SETTING WITH PURPOSE

What do you want this year? In five years? In ten years? When was the last time you've thought about it in detail? What was the last big life goal you set?

Sadly, there are so many people who have long given up on their hopes and dreams. They've thrown in the towel and settled for mediocrity in all areas of their life. They go through the days on autopilot. Those days quickly turn into months. The months quickly turn into years, and next thing they know, decades have passed.

The good news is, if you're reading this book, chances are you are not one of those people. You are in the driver's seat of your life, ready to take control and manifest your wildest dreams. It's never too late to chase your dreams, set a new goal, or change paths.

A Harvard Business School study found that eighty-three percent of people don't set goals, and those who do have goals are ten times more likely to be successful. This shows that the vast majority of people are missing the very first element of the Law of Attraction, which is getting clear on what you want. How can the Universe deliver something you never ask for?

Whenever someone comes to me and says they are having trouble manifesting, I always start by asking them what they want. Almost every time, I get one of the following answers:

* *I want more money.*
* *I want abundance.*
* *I want a perfect relationship.*
* *I want my dream home.*
* *I want a better job.*

I then follow up by asking what that means for them. Does more money mean you want $1,000 more or $1 million more? What does your dream home look like? Describe the details to me. What kind of career do you want?

The majority of the time, I get a vague answer or a deer-in-headlights look and can see that the problem isn't that they can't manifest what they want. The problem is that they don't know what they want.

Everyone thinks they know, but when asked for the details, it becomes tricky. People tend to be wishy-washy. One minute they want a beach house in Florida, and the next minute they want a cabin in the Colorado mountains.

Our mind likes to jump around. It has trouble holding on to a static image and details, so we're left with a vague idea of what we might like. This is far from being crystal clear and makes it almost impossible to visualize.

Be Clear and Specific

When I'm working on goal setting, I like to pretend that I'm ordering from the Universe just like I'm placing an order on Amazon. Imagine trying to find this book on Amazon by typing "book" in the search bar. You'd be left with millions of results to sort through! Even if you typed "nonfiction book" or "manifestation book," there would still be hundreds or maybe even thousands of results to sort through and you may never find this book. It would definitely take longer and be way harder than simply typing "*Trust the Universe*" in the search bar.

This is how specific you should be when placing your order from the Universe. If you were searching for your goal on the internet, it should be clear enough that it would show up in the top results.

When visualizing what you want to manifest, use your five senses to paint a clear picture in your mind. Imagine stepping into that reality. What do you see? Who is with you? How do you feel? What can you smell, taste, or touch? Play it like a movie in your mind and, most importantly, try to tap into the feelings of having it now. This is what will help you align with the frequency of what you want.

Focus on What You Want

Let's look at it from a scientific standpoint. Humans have what's called the Reticular Activating System, or RAS, which is our brain's filter of the overwhelming amount of stimuli we are exposed to every day. It processes what we deem to be important and leaves out the rest. This is why when you

REFRAME
YOUR GOALS

Often, instead of real goals, I just hear a list of all the things people don't want:

I don't want to be in this soul-sucking job anymore.

• • •

I don't want a car that keeps breaking down.

• • •

I don't want friends that cause drama.

Remember, the Law of Attraction is always working, so don't give too much of your thoughts, feelings, and energy to the things you don't want. Instead, practice reframing those things into what you do want:

I want a job that brings me fulfillment.

• • •

I want a new, reliable car.

• • •

I want friends who are supportive and kind.

The good thing about being clear on what you will no longer tolerate is it helps you get really clear on what you are energetically available for. The next time you find your mind wandering to all the things that are no longer serving you, try reframing those things into new goals.

buy something new like a car or talk about something, you all of a sudden start seeing that car everywhere or hearing that topic come up a lot: your brain has tagged it as important and is now processing it for you when it shows up in your environment.

The same goes for opportunities, meeting the right people, and finding the right deals and resources. There's an abundance of opportunities surrounding you at all times, but if you're not focused on your desires and goals, your brain will filter out the corresponding opportunity. If you're focused on the worst-case scenario or fearing your dreams won't come to fruition, your RAS will process the stimuli that correspond with those fears.

You may have heard that what you focus on expands, and this is the science behind why that statement is true. If you're looking for trouble, you'll find it. If you're looking for excuses, you'll find them. If you're looking for success, it will make its way to you. Be mindful of what you focus on the majority of the time and remind yourself that this is the message you're sending to your RAS, which is what will show up in your life.

When you begin to shift your focus from negative to positive or from lack to abundance, you will begin to see more positive, abundant opportunities show up for you. It's not that they didn't exist before. They were always there, but you are now becoming aware of them. The RAS is serving them up to you on a silver platter, but it's up to you to focus on what you want instead of what you don't want.

Practice bringing your awareness to what you're thinking, feeling, talking about, and doing the majority of the time. Awareness will allow you to adjust and reframe anything not serving your highest good.

There Are No Limits

The key is to have fun with this process! There are no rules. There are no limits. The only limits that exist are the limits your mind makes up. You get to set the boundaries of what is possible! Allow yourself to dream big. You're going to manifest anyway, so you might as well focus on manifesting the grandest version of your life.

I have found that the best way to visualize what you want is to put yourself in the scenario of actually having it. Something my husband and I do is go to places that represent our next-level goals. We will get a room at a five-star hotel, purchase tickets to ride on a three-story yacht, or even just grab a drink at a high-end restaurant. The idea is to put ourselves in the scenario of the next level we want to manifest.

I always knew that once I had the money, I wanted to buy a Louis Vuitton handbag. Some people like expensive shoes or cars. My lavish desire is designer luxury handbags. Every time I saw a Louis Vuitton store, I would go in and pretend I was buying my dream luxury handbag.

At first, this felt very uncomfortable. I felt like a fraud. I felt like I didn't belong and I was sure every sales associate knew I couldn't afford to purchase one of their handbags. But two things happened from continuing to put myself in this scenario. First, it helped me get incredibly clear on what I wanted. Seeing the bag on me, feeling it, and the experience of being in this high-end store were much different than trying to visualize these things in my mind. Second, the more I went in there, the more comfortable I felt and the more I began to step into that next-level version of myself that already had the handbag.

If you know you want a new car but don't know what kind, head to some dealerships and start test-driving them. Put yourself in the car. Feel your hands

wrapped around the steering wheel, smell the new car smell, listen to the sound of the engine starting. Whatever it is that you want, give yourself the experience of having it:

* Walk through the model home.
* Try on the shoes.
* Grab a drink in the bar of the five-star hotel.
* Window shop at designer stores.

Have fun with it. Imagine you are browsing through the catalog of the Universe. Pick out what you want. Try it on for a day and see how it feels.

Unwavering Faith

Unwavering faith means having faith long after it seems like it won't manifest. In order to fully believe it will manifest, you must first be absolutely convinced it is a possibility or you won't take the action needed to make it happen. You can do this by visualizing the outcome. Close your eyes and imagine what you want has already happened and you're telling your friend how excited you are that it manifested. Tell them about three obstacles you had to overcome to make it happen. By doing this, you are overcoming the limiting beliefs you hold around this desire. This simple exercise will make your subconscious see the goal as already achieved, so it will no longer doubt whether or not it's possible, and the limiting beliefs will no longer matter. The subconscious doesn't know the difference between reality and fantasy, which is why this is so effective. By thinking you've already made something happen, your subconscious will stop trying to resist it and will now fully believe it's a probability for you.

SETTING
YOUR INTENTION

Give yourself a quick win. If you are new to manifesting, I suggest starting with something small that you want to manifest this week. It can be a cup of coffee, a $10 bill, or anything else that is small enough for you to fully believe you can manifest it. Starting with something small will help you build your manifesting muscle and believe in the process. You can build from there by manifesting bigger goals as you continue seeing proof that the manifestation process works.

Once you get crystal clear on what you want, it's time to set an intention and place your order with the Universe. When I am stating my desire to the Universe, I firmly believe in putting pen to paper. I like to think of it as forging a contract with the Universe. It is declaring what I want. Putting it in ink makes it feel real and tells my mind to stop going back and forth. I've made my decision. This is what I want.

Dear Universe,
I am placing my order for (insert intention).
I am open to receiving guidance in co-creating my reality. I have unwavering faith you will guide me on the path of least resistance. I fully trust the process and surrender control.
Thank you, thank you, thank you!

Feelings are just
visitors, and I can let
them go.

7

HEALING PAST HURTS

Do you want to be in the same exact place next year as you are now? If the answer is no, then you must heal your past hurts and move forward with intention, so you can manifest better.

There are many Law of Attraction teachings that focus on the overall idea of asking, believing, and receiving, but don't dive into the inner work that must be done first. When people have difficulty manifesting, it's usually because of unresolved inner conflict and repressed feelings coupled with limiting beliefs. Until these inner conflicts are resolved, they tend to keep sabotaging you.

As we dive into the inner work, it's important to know that everything, including negative experiences, teaches you something. This can be a good thing, because it helps you get clear on what you don't want and will no longer tolerate. Negative experiences can motivate and empower you to choose better and get intentional in creating your new reality.

It's important to learn from all experiences; however, you must heal the past to keep moving forward and manifest better. Hanging on to the past and reliving your worst moments will only help to attract more similar experiences. If you can move forward with clear intentions, there is no limit to what you can manifest.

Forgiveness

Do you tend to hold grudges against those who wronged you? Forgiveness isn't about them. It's about you. My perspective on forgiveness changed when I heard this quote, sometimes attributed to the Buddha:

"Holding on to anger is like grasping a hot coal with the intent of throwing it at someone else; you are the one that gets burned."

My husband was friends with my brother. When my husband and I started dating, my brother was not okay with it and quit speaking to us. For years, I let it drive me crazy. I was so deeply hurt that every time my brother's name came up, I would well up with anger and frustration. It got to the point that I would miss big family gatherings if he was going to be there. I finally realized that by holding on to this anger, my soul was suffering. I was tired of feeling sadness and anger.

I will never forget the day I decided to forgive him. I declared to the Universe that I was no longer letting this affect me. I sent him good thoughts,

You can call on your spirit guides, higher self, God, or the Universe to help you identify and clear any lingering negative energy. This may even be done subconsciously.

wished him peace, and cut the energetic cord. It felt like the weight of the world lifted off my shoulders. After that, I felt neutral about him and the situation. It no longer ruined my family gatherings or made me uncomfortable. It didn't change the situation or mend our relationship, but I was at peace with it. I could finally drop the negative feelings around it and move on.

What I've come to know is that holding on to grudges is a heavy burden to bear. A common misconception about forgiveness is that it lets the other person off the hook or simply sweeps the issue under the rug. The truth is that forgiveness has very little to do with the other person. It's about giving yourself the freedom to heal and break free from the power that person holds over you. Dwelling on the past will only rob you of peace and the ability to move on to better things. What you don't release will keep showing up in your life.

Just as grudges attract more negativity, so does a desire for revenge. It's important to understand that you cannot use the Law of Attraction to bring harm to others or alter their reality. You are responsible for creating your reality, and yours alone. Remember, whatever energy you put out comes back to you.

If you continue to think about negative experiences, you are actually attracting more experiences like those into your life. In order to break the cycle, you must forgive and let go. Forgive yourself for carrying this heavy burden of past hurts. Letting go of the anger, resentment, and bitterness will clear space for love to come in and make you whole again. It will raise your vibration, opening you up to receive love and abundance.

Releasing Past Relationships

One of the most emotionally charged past hurts has to do with past romantic relationships. When a relationship ends, it typically stirs many strong, negative emotions that are like a powerful electrical charge. This can drastically lower your vibration. Focusing on what went wrong and replaying it in your mind actually makes you a magnet for similar situations. If you want to break free from this harmful pattern, it's time to release the harsh feelings and leave the past where it belongs—in the past. In doing this, you are not letting your partner or ex-partner off the hook. You are not saying what they did was okay. You are simply freeing yourself from the power they still hold over you, so you can manifest better moving forward.

Forgiveness Practice

A powerful Hawaiian practice called "Ho'oponopono" will help you heal past hurts through forgiveness, making you whole again. Take a moment to quiet your mind, come into your heart by placing your hands on your heart, and visualize the people you are forgiving as though they are standing right in front of you. Tell them, "I'm sorry, thank you, I love you, I forgive you."

Saying "I'm sorry" will help you let go of any guilt or shame you're holding on to from the part you played in this. You could be saying sorry to someone else or saying sorry to yourself for holding on to these heavy feelings.

"Thank you" is to give thanks for the lessons that came from this experience. Every experience, even negative ones, teaches you something and contributes to your spiritual growth and understanding.

Love is of the highest vibration. Self-love and sending love to others, even those that have wronged you, is a powerful way to raise your vibration, leave the past in the past, and move forward in a peaceful way that feels good.

By forgiving the person, you now release this past hurt and can move forward with peace and love.

Repeat this practice as many times as you need to until you feel the burden lifted and can let go of the hold this has over you.

Dealing with Toxic Energy

I'm sure you can immediately think of at least one person who has toxic energy. This would be the person who leaves you feeling drained instead of energized. It's the person who is always complaining and looking at the negative in every situation. They may even put you down, make fun of you, or practice some form of mental or emotional abuse.

It's easy to say you will simply cut this person out of your life. But what if this person is a family member, coworker, or longtime friend that you will inevitably see?

I have a simple way of dealing with toxic people. Keep things short, sweet, and surface level. There is no rule that says you have to share everything in your life with everyone. If you know someone isn't supportive or tends to bring up the negative, then don't bare your soul or share your dreams and goals with them. Stick to topics that won't leave you feeling personally attacked. If the conversation turns negative, simply find a way to exit.

MEDITATION

FOR HEALING PAST HURTS

I forgive myself and others for any past hurts. I release their power over me and return to my natural state of love. I move forward with intention and clarity. I am no longer the victim of circumstance. I am the creator of my reality. I choose to activate my heart coherence and step into my higher power.

If you leave every time toxic people get negative, you are teaching them that you won't tolerate negativity. They'll eventually give up and pester someone else. You teach people how to treat you with what you allow.

To take it a step further, what if instead of allowing them to dominate the energy and turn things negative, you turned things positive? Have you ever been around those people who are always smiling and laughing? When you're around them you can't help but smile and feel good. You can be that person! When you're so high vibe, one of two things will happen. Low-vibe people will naturally fall back, or your vibe will raise theirs and you will leave them feeling good and optimistic. Remember, love is the highest vibration, and you can spread it in a simple conversation. "I love your outfit! I love this food! I love that we got a chance to hang out!" It seems simple because it is. Focus on the good, and you will attract the good in others.

Here's the bottom line. People living their best life and holding a high vibration are not going to go out of their way to knock you down. It's the people who are hurting, who are stuck in victim mode and holding a lower vibration that feel the need to attack another person. Your positivity makes them uncomfortable because they are in a bad place and aren't yet ready to shift. When you view it like that, it's easier to see them from a place of empathy and compassion, send them healing vibes, and keep doing your thing.

As the famous Jim Rohn quote goes, "You are the average of the five people you spend the most time with." You mirror who is around you the most. This is when mirror neurons fire in our brain. This is why we yawn when we see someone else yawning. You will begin to pick up on the language, mannerisms, attitudes, and beliefs of the people you are around the most. If you hang around people who are always complaining and gossiping, chances are you will become a complainer and gossiper. If you hang around people who are focused on self-improvement, chances are you will become focused on self-improvement as well.

Write about the following questions in your journal to gain some perspective on your inner circle:

* Who do you spend the most time with?
* Who is in your close circle?
* Are they supporting your dreams or contradicting them?
* Are their goals similar to yours?
* Are they holding you back or making you feel bad or ashamed for aiming high?
* Are they leaving you feeling energized or drained?

If you find that your circle is not meeting your needs, manifest a supportive circle of friends. What types of people inspire you? In what ways would you like them to support you? What goals and interests would you like to share?

Breaking the Energetic Cord

Another effective practice that you can try at the end of the day, or anytime you feel someone sucking the energy out of you, is to break the energetic cord.

Energetic cords are created between you and people you come in contact with. They flow between your energy fields, transferring emotional energy.

Sit down and focus on your breath. Go inward and ask yourself if there is anyone with an energetic cord connected to you that may be leaving you feeling drained, negative, or just off. Visualize this cord running from their field of energy to yours. Now imagine a pair of scissors cutting the cord and freeing you from their energy.

That's it. You can do this as often as you need to. Initially, you may have many cords to cut if you are new to this practice. I recommend doing this daily before you go to bed to free yourself from anyone you encountered during the day.

SENDING LOVE
MEDITATION

As you know by now, love and gratitude are high-vibrational feelings. One of the most powerful things you can do to heal past hurts with others is to send them love and gratitude.

Sit down with your back straight
and begin focusing on your breathing. No need to alter it. Just bring awareness to it. Now imagine a bright, golden light coming down from the Universe through your crown chakra and filling your body with this light, which is pure loving and healing energy.

Place your hands on your heart
and imagine this energy collecting into a big, powerful ball of light at your heart. You can take this ball and extend it outward to anyone. In doing this, you are sending them this powerful, healing, and loving energy. They may not realize it or understand it, but they can surely feel it.

This is an incredible way to send love and peace to anyone, including those you've had conflict with. It symbolizes you releasing them in a loving and peaceful way.

This exercise is also a reminder that we are all interconnected and you have access to this unconditional love anytime you need. You are so loved and supported by the Universe. You can immerse yourself in this love anytime you need to. It's always available no matter what. It is your natural state. It is the core of who you are. It's always present.

Today will be
a positive day filled
with joy.

CHAPTER 8

PRACTICING POSITIVE DAILY HABITS

The number one excuse people give for not making lasting positive changes in their life is that they don't have enough time. Have you ever found yourself saying, "I would work out, but I don't have enough time" or "I'd love to start meditating, but I don't have time"? What if I told you a life beyond your wildest dreams was possible if you dedicated fifteen minutes of your time to it every day? Would you be able to find the time?

The issue really isn't time. It's that we aren't prioritizing our time. We give so much of our time to mindless tasks. Think about how many minutes per day you spend watching TV, checking email, scrolling on social media, or talking to friends and coworkers who gossip or complain. We trade the majority of our time for money and yet we won't dedicate fifteen minutes of our day to our life goals. We have it all backwards. There is plenty of time when you shift your focus from the things draining your energy to the things that feed your soul.

I used to wake up every morning to the sound of my alarm taking me from my blissful dream world into a state of complete dread thinking about the day ahead. I would usually hit the snooze button only to wake up ten minutes later in a state of panic knowing I'd have to rush to make up that time. I'd hurry around the house trying to get myself and my daughter ready so we could get to work and school on time. I would feel flustered and cranky. As I drove through the morning traffic, my anxiety would continue to grow with the words of my first manager racing in the back of my mind: "If you're early, you're on time. If you're on time, you're late. If you're late, don't even bother showing up."

This hectic routine continued for over a decade. The stress and anxiety were taking a toll on me. Desperate to find balance in my life, I began researching positive habits to combat stress and anxiety. I began learning about meditation and the scientific research proving its powerful effects on managing stress, anxiety, and a variety of other health issues.

I read that meditating for just three minutes per day relieved stress, so I started doing that over my lunch break. Normally, I'd return to work in a post-lunch groggy state, needing an espresso to get me through the rest of the day. After I started meditating, I began feeling completely refocused and re-energized. It felt like the equivalent of taking a nice, long nap and waking up feeling refreshed. It was as if all my lingering questions were answered with clarity. It was then that I realized that meditating gave me time back. It allowed

As I do the inner work to raise my vibration, I attract more high-vibrational experiences into my life. Every day is filled with joy, love, and gratitude.

me to tap into that inner wisdom and state of creative flow, making the rest of the work day feel effortless. Instead of mindlessly going through the motions, I was working with creativity, precision, and focus. I realized that one brilliant idea that came to me during meditation could save me years of wasted time staying in a situation that wasn't aligned with my purpose.

Start Your Day Right

As I continued on my personal growth journey, I realized that how I was starting my day was negatively impacting my mindset first thing in the morning, which affected my entire day. I started setting my alarm clock ten minutes earlier and used those ten minutes to focus on my well-being.

This had such a big impact on my mindset and the way I felt that I began researching the most effective morning habits. As I got into a new morning routine, I began waking up filled with enthusiasm and joy. It changed my entire outlook for the day and work week and eventually my life as a whole.

Here's what I incorporated into my mornings. Try each of these elements out and see which works best for you. Feel free to make this your own. There is no right way to create a morning routine. It looks different for everyone, so trust what feels good to you. Keep in mind, the first couple of weeks may feel tough as you're getting used to it, so start slow and give it some time before deciding if it's for you or not.

MOVEMENT: Start your morning by getting out of bed and doing five minutes of stretching and light yoga. Get the blood circulating to wake up your body and set an intention for your day. Movement helps you get out of your head and come into your heart. It moves the stagnant energy, so creative ideas can flow.

ALERTNESS: To get out of a groggy state, brush your teeth, wash your face or shower, and drink a glass of water.

MEDITATION AND VISUALIZATION: Take at least two minutes every morning and evening to visualize your big-picture dream while feeling all the feelings of having it now. It's amazing how powerful this two-minute practice is.

GRATITUDE: Give gratitude every morning. Gratitude is at the center of the Law of Attraction. This is the easiest and fastest way to get in a high-vibrational state. If you want to attract more positive things in your life, you must be grateful for what you already have.

GO OUTDOORS: Syncing with nature helps you get in touch with your higher self and feel connected to all that is. Instead of doing, just be. Slow down and come into your heart. This is where you will filter out all of the unnecessary stuff and get in touch with your intuition.

Shake Up the Energy

While it's important to tip the scales to the positive side, you are still a human being and will still feel the wide array of human emotions, both good and bad. No one can be positive all the time. This is something often promoted in spiritual circles and on social media and can be harmful because it can cause people to bury emotions rather than processing them. It can also lead you to feel guilt or shame around experiencing anger, rage, or sadness. No one is exempt from these emotions. It's important to allow yourself to feel what you're feeling and release the feelings rather than repressing them and letting them build up inside of you. Here are some ways to release these emotions:

Start by setting your alarm clock just ten minutes early and pick one practice to integrate into your morning routine.

VENTING: Verbally expressing what's bothering you can be very therapeutic. Venting your frustrations with a thera-pist, counselor, or trusted friend can help you move through those emotions, so you can move forward with clarity. If venting to a friend, make sure they are willing and able to listen, so you don't drain them energetically.

MOVEMENT: When you're feeling down, the last thing you probably want to do is get up and move, but shaking up the energy in your body is a very quick and effective way to release pent-up emotions and raise your vibration. Exercise, dancing, and even going for a walk will move that negative energy out, leaving you feeling renewed.

Positive Practices to Raise Your Vibration

The following suggestions can help you tip the scales back to the positive when you need it:

SMILING: Did you know that smiling releases feel-good hormones in your body? Even if it's forced, it still works. Smiling is also contagious. Test it out. Pick someone who looks like they're having a bad day and smile at them. I guarantee you'll get a smile back, and that one simple smile will probably change their entire day!

RANDOM ACTS OF KINDNESS: You will get just as much joy out of giving as receiving. Whether it's buying someone's lunch, holding the door open, or leaving money for someone to find, there are so many ways you can make a difference. These small acts have a ripple effect that extends far beyond what you can imagine.

LAUGHTER: As they say, laughter is the best medicine. You can't help but feel good after a good laugh. Watch a funny movie and allow yourself to lighten up. Don't sweat the small stuff. Instead, laugh it off.

FEEL-GOOD MUSIC: Music is a guaranteed way to feel better. Create a feel-good playlist or listen to a song that brings back good memories.

We have so many simple yet powerful tools at our disposal for feeling good. It's amazing so many people stay stuck in a negative mindset or feeling mediocre at best. Why feel okay when you can feel great?

Remember, your most dominant feelings determine your vibration. The better you feel, the higher your vibration. The higher your vibration, the more you will attract high-vibrational experiences into your life.

Start thinking about what leaves you feeling high vibe and try to incorporate that into your routine more often.

MAKE MANIFESTATION

A HABIT

Our subconscious is controlling the show the majority of the time. This is why it's so hard to form new habits or quit old habits. This is why people read a self-improvement book and get all excited to change their life but end up right back in their normal routine two days later without making any meaningful progress.

Here are some practices that will help you integrate intentional manifestation into your daily life:

Question everything. This will help you bring awareness to your limiting beliefs and anything holding you back in your subconscious.

• • •

Check in with your thoughts and feelings throughout the day to see where your focus and energy are going.

• • •

Hold the vision of what you want to manifest twice a day for two minutes.

• • •

Allow yourself to dream big and let your imagination run wild. Make gratitude a constant in your life.

• • •

Practice manifesting little things to build up your belief in the process.

• • •

Keep your vision front and center. Journal about it, create a vision board, and leave sticky notes or reminders with affirmations.

I am
safe and loved.

RECEIVING AND EMBRACING YOUR DESIRES

....

Open your heart, and you open yourself to receiving all that you desire. An open heart clears the way for abundance to flow into every area of your life. It heals, awakens, and empowers you to step into your higher self.

As we go through life, disappointments, heartbreaks, and hurtful moments can cause us to protect our hearts by putting up a barrier. It may be difficult for us to accept love, compliments, and positive gestures. We feel like if we keep love out, we are saving ourselves from the pain of heartbreaks and disappointments. The truth of the matter is that keeping love out will not save you from feeling pain or getting hurt. Instead, it blocks your heart chakra, which can prevent you from making deep connections with people, having thriving relationships, and receiving your desires.

You may be thinking, *Of course I want love, abundance, and to receive my desires!* Wanting something and being open to receiving it are two different things. You may consciously want something, but if it contradicts your subconscious beliefs, you will subconsciously close yourself off from receiving it. For example, if you want to manifest money, but have a subconscious belief that people with money are bad or dishonest, your subconscious will sabotage you from attracting money to keep you safe from becoming bad or dishonest. If you want to manifest a romantic relationship, but you have the subconscious belief that all relationships lead to heartbreak, your subconscious will block love to keep you safe from heartache.

Recognizing a Block

Signs you are blocked from receiving love can be found in how you accept help, gifts, and compliments. When someone pays you a compliment, do you smile and say thank you or do you try to diminish the compliment by saying something negative about yourself? When someone offers to help you, do you accept the help or do you feel bad about asking for help? Do you feel shame around wanting what you want? Do you have trouble asking for what you desire?

I had set an income goal a few years back and told myself when I reached that goal, I'd buy myself a Louis Vuitton bag, which was something I'd dreamed of having for years. It symbolized success for me. I picked out the bag I wanted and visualized it all the time. Yet when I reached the income goal, I couldn't bring myself to buy the bag. I kept thinking of all the things we could do with that money that the whole family could enjoy, like a vacation or buying something for the house. That was the problem. I had no problem

Love is my natural state.
I am tapped into the
frequency of love, and I give
and receive love freely. I
love myself unconditionally.

buying big things for others. I just couldn't do the same for myself. I actually made my husband buy it for me as a birthday gift.

What this was doing was sending a message to the Universe that I was not open to receiving. It was giving off the vibration of not being worthy of receiving big things for myself. It was affirming that the only way I could have nice things was if they came as gifts.

That's when I realized that all the big-picture goals for my life were never going to come to fruition unless I worked through this belief that I didn't deserve to spend money on myself. How would I continue pursuing goals if I never celebrated or rewarded the incremental wins along the way?

Learning to Be Open

I began looking at things differently. I thought of the message I was sending to my kids. I want them to know they are worthy of everything they want in life. I want them to take care of themselves and treat themselves with unconditional love. But as we know, kids learn from watching their parents, so I knew I'd have to start showing myself the same level of love and worthiness.

I had to remind myself that being open to receiving isn't selfish. When you allow yourself to accept your desires, you are showing up better for those around you. Reward yourself, pamper yourself, and love yourself, so that you can be the best version of you for the ones you love.

It's time to crack yourself wide open to receiving all you desire. By keeping yourself blocked from receiving your desires, you are keeping yourself in a state of lack. Opening yourself up allows you to shift from a lack mindset to one of abundance. When you go through life with an open heart, you open the floodgates for abundance, love, and receiving your desires from the Universe.

The key to opening yourself up to receiving is raising your vibrational frequency to that of love. You can access the frequency of love anytime by practicing gratitude. Gratitude is essentially giving love for the things in your life. As you go about your day, try to find as many things as possible to give love and gratitude for, even the little things. *I love this cup of coffee! I love the weather today! I love this outfit!* Try to really feel it deeply. The more you feel something, the more powerful it is in changing your vibrational frequency.

Your Heart Chakra

Your heart chakra is the center of all chakras; therefore, many feel it is the most powerful chakra. It is the bridge between your emotions and spirituality. Signs that your heart chakra is blocked can include holding grudges, difficulty connecting with others, difficulty in relationships, and feelings like anger, rage, and jealousy. As we discussed in chapter seven, forgiveness is essential to healing. Once you can forgive, you can move forward in the healing process by opening up your heart chakra.

Nothing is more powerful in opening your heart chakra than self-love. How you love yourself determines how you will manifest love in your life. So often, we can be our own worst enemies. If we make a mistake or do something embarrassing, we are overly harsh on ourselves and not very forgiving. When we look in the mirror, we can be extremely critical of the way we look.

When you give gratitude first thing in the morning, you are priming your mindset to be more optimistic for the rest of the day.

Think of some of the negative self-talk that comes up for you and write it down. Now I want you to read it out loud and pretend you are reading it to your best friend. Would you ever talk to your best friend that way? Of course not. So why allow yourself to go there?

Self-love is about getting back to your default state of love before the world filled you with beliefs and perceptions that you're not enough. How many times have you thought that you were not pretty enough, skinny enough, young enough, old enough, experienced enough, smart enough, or outgoing enough?

Those are all stories we tell ourselves based on our perceptions of the world around us. The truth is you are enough! You have always been enough and always will be enough just as you are.

We go through this programming as children when we are made to believe we should fit in and be just like everyone else. We learn to dull our unique qualities or hide them away. Imagine how boring life would be if we all liked the same things and thought the same way. There would never be innovation or excitement in life. It would be dull and mediocre. In fact, look at all the people throughout history that you admire. Most people that made history and changed the world did not fit the mold. They went against the grain. They were different and instead of hiding their uniqueness, they embraced it. They followed the things that lit them up even if society judged them for it.

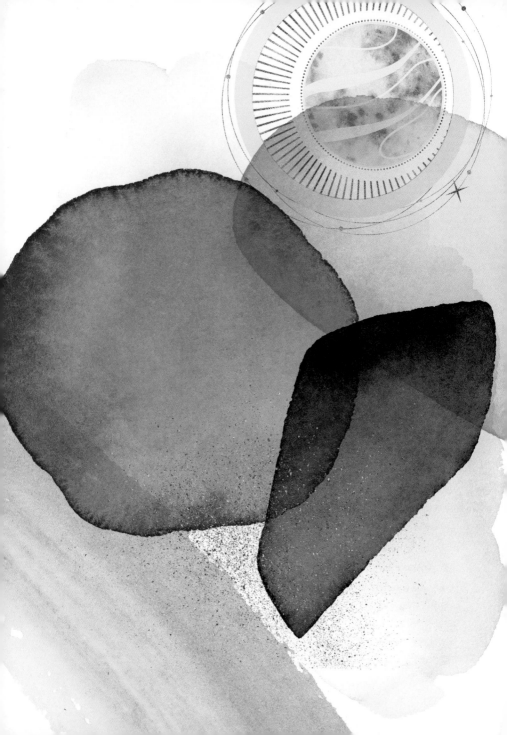

There are people that are waiting to see the real, authentic you. They need your gifts. The world doesn't need another carbon copy. The world needs to see the things that make you different. Embrace those things. Give love for all the things that make you different.

Mirror Work

Most women have battled feeling self-conscious about their looks at one point or another. Our society likes to make women feel like they never measure up with their weight or beauty. Beauty ads, celebrities, and social media reaffirm that we must meet some external criteria to be considered pretty enough, skinny enough, or just enough in general. Try to go back as far as you can and find the moment where you first began feeling self-conscious.

For me, it was when I was in elementary school and my friend made fun of my weight. I shrugged it off until her mom chimed in and confirmed that I weighed much more than her daughter. Hearing it from an adult and the tone that she used made me feel like I was inferior because of the number on the scale. It was the first time I began looking at the scale and feeling like I had to adjust the way I looked in order to be loved and accepted by others. From that moment forward, I became obsessed with how much I weighed and began the comparison game where I equated my self-worth with the number on the scale.

The next moment was in sixth grade when I landed the lead role in a class play. I felt so proud of myself until the mean girl in school came up to me and said, "Stephanie, how did you land the lead part? She's supposed to be played by someone pretty, and you aren't." To this day, I can still feel how my cheeks instantly went hot and my eyes welled up with tears. It was the first time anyone suggested I wasn't enough because of the way I looked. That was when I began scrutinizing myself in the mirror and began wearing makeup to cover up what I thought were imperfections.

We all have stories like this. You may laugh and think those little moments are no big deal and just a part of growing up. But they are a seed that continually gets watered throughout your life with the messaging and expectations of society around how we *should* be instead of just accepting ourselves as we already are.

That changes today. Today, you are going to start accepting the real you. You will begin to love your so-called imperfections and realize they make you unique. You will start showing yourself the love and acceptance that society never gave you. This is where mirror work comes in.

Mirror work feels really awkward and silly at first. You will probably try to skip this activity, but trust me, it is one of the most powerful things you can do to begin chipping away at the damage those moments did to your self-esteem.

Go in the bathroom, lock the door so you can have privacy, and just try it. Stand in front of the mirror, gaze into your eyes, and say "I love you" over and over again until you feel love wash over you and open your heart. List all the things you love about yourself. Show yourself the love and acceptance that you didn't get during those hard moments in your life. When is the last time you truly looked at yourself in the mirror in a loving and kind way? When was the last time you gave yourself a compliment instead of pointing out every imperfection? When you feel good about yourself, you radiate positivity.

WRITE A LOVE LETTER
TO YOURSELF

List all the qualities that make you unique. What do people always compliment you on? What things do people come to you for help with? What are you proud of yourself for? What have you had the power to overcome? Write it all down! Don't be bashful. The only person that will see this is you, so let your heart go wild with all the wonderful things you embody!

• • •

HEART CHAKRA
MEDITATION

Sit in meditation with your eyes closed and your hands placed on your heart. Begin focusing on your breathing and allow your body to relax. Imagine a green light flowing down through your head to your heart. Continue to bring awareness to this green light nurturing your heart chakra, opening it up like a lotus flower, and filling you with love.

I attract my desires with ease.

MANIFESTING WITH AN OPEN HEART

....

There is one key to the Law of Attraction. It unlocks the door to manifesting anything you want effortlessly. It is the core of who we are. It's our natural state. The key is love.

Love is the highest vibration we can attain. It is what gives mothers superhuman strength when their children are in harm's way. It's what causes life to continue. Without it, we would cease to exist. Love is the vibration of creation.

Since love is the highest vibration, it is what helps us manifest quickly and effortlessly. Holding on to the feeling and vibration of love will make you a magnet for all you desire.

Your ego works to keep you in your safe bubble. It's time to break free. You do this by getting out of your head and coming into your heart.

Your higher self comes from a place of pure love. Ask yourself, *What would she do? What would she say? How would she be?* This allows you to become one with her.

Activating Heart Coherence

Did you know your heart has its own electrical system? It is a powerful energy center and can communicate with the brain and the electromagnetic field around you. When you come into a state of heart coherence, you are accessing this powerful energy and using it to impress your desires on the electromagnetic field around you, aligning yourself to the frequency of manifesting your desires.

Activating heart coherence may sound complicated, but it is quite simple. It requires immersing yourself in the present moment and looking within rather than focusing on the external environment.

* Begin by closing your eyes and placing your hand on your heart.
* Focus on your breathing and allow yourself to relax.
* Imagine a ball of light emanating from your heart and connecting with the light force around you.
* Visualize your desires as already manifested and tap into the feelings of love, joy, and gratitude.
* As you feel these heart-based feelings, see this light grow brighter.

By embodying the emotions of that which you wish to manifest, that light force around you will match with the energetic state of those heart-centered emotions, causing a shift from one reality to another, also known as quantum manifesting.

I am so grateful my desires
are already on their way to
me. Thank you for delivering
everything in divine timing.

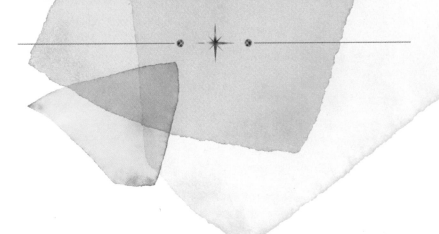

Quantum Manifesting

One theory of quantum physics is that there is an infinite number of parallel realities. They are right beside us in a different frequency. Just as you can switch the radio and tune into another channel, you can tune into different frequencies. This is done by embodying the feelings of having it now. Acting as if you have already obtained your desires and most importantly *feeling* the feelings of having them already is how this shift occurs. Your heart is the energetic conduit by which this is possible. Visualizing what you want while feeling it is activating brain-heart coherence. This manipulates the energy field that surrounds you, allowing for quantum manifesting to take place.

Being in the present moment is the best way to quickly activate brain-heart coherence. A simple practice to bring your awareness to the present is to focus on your breathing. The easiest way to tap into the feelings of having your desires now is through gratitude. Give love and gratitude for it now as though it's already yours. These simple things are a powerful way to make the quantum shift. The more you do it, the more it becomes second nature and your life becomes better than you ever thought possible.

A quick way to activate heart coherence

is to simply place your hand on your heart and visualize the energy surrounding it.

BREATHING

EXERCISES

If you find it difficult to focus on the present moment,
try one of these breathing exercises:

4-7-8 BREATHING

Inhale for four counts, hold for seven counts,
and exhale for eight counts. Repeat.

COHERENT BREATHING

Inhale for five counts, exhale for five counts. Repeat.

TRIANGLE BREATHING

Inhale through your nose for three counts, hold for three
counts, and exhale through your mouth for three counts.

My life is
abundant and full of
opportunities.

11

FINDING
YOUR PURPOSE

When I'm discussing life goals with people, I often get asked what they should do if they have no idea what their purpose is. This is common. We go through childhood and young adulthood being conditioned by our parents and teachers to go down one specific path. We are programmed to believe if we get good grades, we can go to a good college and get a good job that pays well and has good benefits, and then we will be happy. This dream that we are fed is missing an important question. What will actually make us happy and leave us feeling fulfilled? Your parents, teachers, and society mean well, but only you can truly discover your soul's purpose. Without it, you may feel unfulfilled, restless, or energetically drained.

Have you ever looked at people driving in morning traffic? So many are in a zombie-like state, simply going through the motions and living the same day over and over again. They are on autopilot because they never questioned the path society laid out for them. They only looked outside for guidance rather than going inward. They tell themselves all kinds of excuses for why they don't feel fulfilled:

* Life is hard.
* Suck it up.
* This is the safe path. Anything else is scary and unknown, so I better stay put.
* I'm fine.

Fine is not great. Don't settle for a mediocre life just because someone told you it's the safe path. You weren't put here to simply exist. You were put here to live, learn, grow, and thrive! Are you thriving? Or are you existing?

If you are feeling restless or frustrated with your job, relationship, or life in general, it is because your higher self sees another more fulfilling path or easier way. This is when you need to pay attention. Listen to your intuition. Follow those subtle nudges you get. This is the Universe communicating with you and guiding you toward your purpose.

This is how you discover your soul's true calling. The answer will not be found in asking your family, friends, neighbors, teachers, or coaches. The answer can only be found within you.

Your desires are placed in you for a reason. They are clues that can lead you to your purpose. So often, people feel guilty or ashamed for desiring something. You may feel greedy or outlandish for wanting something outside of your familiar comfort zone. There is no shame in wanting what you want. Pay attention to your desires and ask yourself questions. If you were to fulfill these desires, how would your life be different? What would you be doing differently?

Spirit guides of the highest love and compassion, please help shine a light on what it is I am here to do. What do you need me to know? What do you need me to see?

Forget the How

As stated earlier, your intuition is your inner guidance system. It knows the most fulfilling path. Chances are you are tuning it out. It's time to slow down and reconnect with your inner antenna. Get out a journal or meditate and ask for guidance. Allow yourself to be fully open to whatever comes through without judgment. Don't try to make sense of it or figure out how your desires will manifest. Your conscious mind is very limited in seeing all the different options available to you. Let your higher self handle that part. Stay focused on the outcome and have unwavering faith in the Universe to deliver it.

Tap into Your Creativity

Most adults would say they are not creative. This is simply not true. We are all born creative. As children, we are always tapped into a state of creative flow because we haven't yet been conditioned to believe that creativity is a waste of time or creativity doesn't pay the bills. Just look at young children. They let their imagination run wild without worrying about whether it's reasonable. They draw and paint and don't worry about whether it meets societal standards. They sing and dance because it feels good. They don't worry about judgment from others.

Somewhere along the way, we hide our creativity. We realize it makes us vulnerable to judgment. We dull our sparkle and work really hard to fit in. The truth is, we all are creative beings and no matter how hard you tuck away your creativity, it is still there resting and waiting for you to rediscover it.

The key is to do this with no other purpose than to have fun and enjoy the process.

The good news is you can tap into your creativity at any time. What did you love doing as a child? Coloring, painting, dancing, making crafts? Do that now! Don't worry about the end product or worry about anyone else's judgment. In fact, you can even get creative in the privacy of your own home. No one needs to know or see your creative projects. This is for you. It's about having fun and feeling free to create just for the sake of creating. In doing so, you will find yourself getting back into a state of creative flow where time doesn't work the same. It's a state of fun and play that adults don't allow themselves to enjoy very often.

It's in this state that you become one with the Universe and are divinely guided to your purpose. Your purpose may have nothing to do with the creative project you're working on, but the simple act of creating opens you up to co-create with the Universe and makes you a clear channel for guidance to flow through.

Find Your Why

You may think you already know your life's purpose, but I challenge you to dig a little deeper and make sure you know *why* you want this. Have you chosen a particular path because it lights you up or is it simply a means to an end? Have you actually chosen it or has someone else, like your parents, teachers, or society?

A simple exercise to help you get to your why is to continue asking why until you no longer have an answer.

When I first learned about the Law of Attraction, I wanted to manifest promotions at my company and climb my way up the corporate ladder. The problem is that every promotion left me feeling more stressed and took more and more time away from my family.

When I started to dig deeper and ask myself why I wanted these promotions, I found that I wanted to make more money. When I asked myself why I wanted more money, I thought that the money would allow me to pay my house off. When I asked why I wanted to pay the house off, the answer was so that I could stay home and raise my daughter, and by paying the house off, I could afford to quit my job. The real purpose I was after was to quit my job and stay home with my daughter, which is the exact opposite of the promotions I was manifesting. I was focusing on the thing I didn't want because my subconscious had some twisted belief about that being the only path that would allow me to stay home with my daughter. I was not aligned with my true purpose, which is why I was feeling unfulfilled. Was there another way to stay with my daughter? A way that would allow me to fulfill my purpose? Of course! But I had closed myself off from any other possibility by focusing on how I thought it had to happen. Drop the how and focus on your why.

JOURNAL PROMPTS

Here are some questions to ask yourself when you find yourself
wanting something just because it's a means to an end:

What is the end result you're after?

• • •

If you knew you couldn't fail, what would you try?

• • •

*If you knew you wouldn't be judged by
others, what would you do?*

• • •

If you had unlimited funds, what would you do?

I release fear
and open myself
to love.

12

RISING ABOVE FEAR

Is it your dreams or fears that are guiding your life? Fear paralyzes you from taking action toward your dreams. It keeps you small. We are programmed by our society to fear failure. Our entire schooling system is set up around testing. We are taught that failing is bad. It means you're not smart or won't make it in life. It's something we are taught to fear, and it creates a lot of limiting beliefs that hold us back in life. But imagine what your own life might be like if you began looking differently at failure.

J.K. Rowling was rejected by all twelve publishers she sent the first *Harry Potter* manuscript to. She didn't give up, and eventually a small publisher accepted her work and she became one of the richest women in the world, donating massive amounts to charity and giving the world a book series that would be enjoyed by millions for years to come.

Henry Ford had two companies that went bankrupt before forming the automobile company that produced the Model T, revolutionizing the automobile industry.

Oprah Winfrey was fired from her first television job because the producer felt she was unfit for television. She went on to host one of the most popular television shows in history and started her own network, touching the lives of millions of people all over the globe.

There are countless stories just like these. Almost anyone who is successful that you admire has likely faced many challenges, failures, and great risks. Imagine if they had let fear stop them. Life would be different, not just for them, but for the millions of people their inspired action impacted. They all took a very different approach to what we are taught. They held a clear vision of what they wanted to manifest and knew that the road to success and fulfillment is often paved with "failures." But they realized those aren't really failures in the way we are taught. They are simply detours from the Universe that direct you onto a better path. They believed in their vision with such unwavering faith that no matter what rejection they faced, they persevered. They held the faith long after it looked like it would never happen. They were able to do this because they were tapped into their higher self and listened to their intuition to access the inspired thoughts and action steps needed to bring their dreams to fruition.

Imagine what the world could be like if we taught this concept to children instead of instilling fear around failure.

Fear of Judgment

The fear of judgment can hold us back from sharing our true self with the world. Chances are you had moments in your childhood where you were bullied in some way or you witnessed someone else being bullied and you protected yourself by blending in. You were taught that if you fit in with

My dreams are
bigger than my fears.
The world needs what I have
to offer. I am calling
upon the Universe to give me
guidance and the
courage to take the
next step.

everyone else, you will be accepted and loved and if you stood out in some way, embarrassment and pain would follow.

As you go through life, this little seed of fear around judgment is always in the back of your mind, oftentimes affecting your daily life without you even realizing it. Maybe you water down your social media posts so people won't think you're being too blunt. You don't want to offend anyone, so you may hold back from sharing your true opinion. Perhaps you stop yourself from wearing the outfit or jewelry you love because it may come across as too much: too extravagant, too eccentric, too sexy. You may hold back from attaining the things you really want because you are worried people will think you're greedy or selfish. The opposite may also be true. Maybe you feel like you're boring or not enough, so you stress about keeping up with the Joneses.

The people who do judge you are going to judge you regardless, so you may as well do what you really want and let them judge for you that. I once came across a social media post that said something along these lines:

* In your teens and twenties, you worry about what everyone else thinks.
* In your thirties and forties, you begin to accept yourself and quit worrying what others think.
* In your fifties and sixties, you realize everyone else was so caught up in their own world, they were never thinking about you in the first place.

There's so much truth to that. People are focused on their own lives, their own dreams, and their own insecurities. In fact, when someone judges you, they are actually reflecting their own insecurities onto you. There may be moments of judgment here and there you will undoubtedly face, but the vast majority of the time, people are in their own world, not focusing on you. People may judge you for something embarrassing you said or something "bad" you did, but moments later they will forget all about it and move on to something else.

It's time to stop letting this fear of judgment keep a hold over you and start living your life and shining your light according to you—the real, authentic you.

Fear of Rejection

We have all had that moment in our past where we were rejected. Maybe you asked someone out and they said no or maybe you asked your parents for a toy you really wanted and were immediately told no and made to feel bad for even asking. These seemingly small life events in our childhood have a way of sticking with us into adulthood, making it really scary to ask for what we want. You had your ego bruised before. You associated some hard feelings with that and now your subconscious is working really hard to make sure that never happens to you again. But what are you missing out on? Worst-case scenario, you are told no. If that's the case, you are no worse off than you are right now. Sure, your ego may be a little bruised, but you have likely gained some knowledge or perspective along the way. Best-case scenario, you get what you want! Don't let fear of rejection stand between you and what you want to manifest.

Fear of Failure

The mind has a way of making the worst-case scenario seem worse than it really is and usually downplays the best-case scenario, leaving you with the feeling of *better be safe than sorry*.

I remember being at a crossroads in my life where I wanted to leave my "safe" corporate job and pursue my purpose of teaching people all over the globe about the Law of Attraction. I knew in my heart what I truly wanted, yet the thought of leaving my job terrified me. My mind was blowing the worst-case scenario way out of proportion, telling me that if things didn't work out, I was doomed. I would lose everything. One day I was listening to a podcast and they were talking about a survey that was done with people at the end of life. They said that people tended to regret the things they *didn't* do, not the things they *did* do. Then it dawned on me that the worst-case scenario wasn't trying and failing. After all, if I did completely fail, I could always go find another mediocre sales job. The real worst-case scenario was never even trying and ending up filled with regrets at the end of life. The best-case scenario was making all of my wildest dreams come true! Isn't that worth the risk of failing? That was the moment I decided I would pursue my dreams, and I haven't looked back since.

Taking action will help you get out of your head and put your manifestation into motion.

Overcoming Fear and Anxiety with Visualization

I have dealt with anxiety my whole life. Not realizing it, I used the Law of Attraction as a child to overcome it by visualizing the outcome I wanted. Growing up, I was very shy. When I had to give a speech in school, it terrified me to the point that I would feel sick. Before I gave the speech, I would visualize myself with confidence in front of the class. I would picture capturing everyone's attention. I would visualize my teacher giving me an A. While I didn't realize I was manifesting, I did know that it helped me get through the scary moments in life. I knew that when I visualized my desired outcome, things always seemed to work in my favor.

After 9/11, I developed a fear of flying. Whenever I would fly on a plane, before takeoff, I would close my eyes and visualize the plane landing safely on the runway. I would feel relief wash over me and give gratitude for the safe flight. I had unwavering faith that by holding that vision, all would be well, and it would expel any anxiety I had about being on a plane.

Inspired Action

Most people doubt their intuition and just fantasize about taking action toward their dreams someday. Those fulfilling their purpose trust their intuition and take inspired action *now*. The best way to overcome your fears is by taking action. Have you ever heard the saying "strike while the iron's hot"? This applies to manifesting as well. When you have an inspired idea, understand that it's coming through at that exact moment for a reason. The Universe has divine timing and is planting that seed of inspiration in you because it's the perfect time to take action. Oftentimes, we get inspired ideas and we tell ourselves we will come back to them later. The problem is, we almost never do. We completely forget about them. The more time that goes by, the more time our mind has to convince us it's a bad idea by coming up with all the ways it could go wrong and reaffirming all our limiting beliefs. Even if you do try to take action later, it's not going to have the same result, because you won't have the same creative energy flowing through you that you did the moment you received the idea. Trust the Universe and leap into action.

When you feel paralyzed from taking action, a simple and quick trick for overcoming fear and anxiety is to shake up the energy in your body. This will help you get out of your head and come into your body. Literally shake your body, starting with your head, arms, and hands, and work your way all the way down to your legs and feet and feel the anxiety dissolve.

Surrender and Let Go

How do you visualize and embody your desires while also surrendering and letting go of the outcome? This is a question I get a lot. It all has to do with your energy and vibration. Visualizing and thinking about your desires should feel good. It should feel exciting and fun. If you find yourself feeling uncertain, doubting it will happen, and thinking you have to constantly focus and visualize your goals or else they won't manifest, that is fear-based thinking and having the opposite effect from what you intend. When you are coming from a place of desperation, doubt, or fear, you are actually repelling the very thing you are trying to manifest.

Imagine going on a date with someone and having a great time, then agreeing you will go on a second date the following week. You think you like this person and you're excited to see them again. You're thinking it could possibly turn into a relationship. Now imagine, this person calls you later that night just to check in and make sure you had a good time and still wants to meet up next week. Then the next day, they call again and say, "I know you said you wanted to meet up next week, but I just wanted to call and make sure you still want to." Then they keep calling over and over again to confirm that you had a good time and like them and want to see them again. By the second or third call, you'd be running for the hills thinking this person is a crazy stalker! Desperation and lack of confidence is a repellent.

Have complete faith the Universe will deliver your desires just as you have complete confidence the Amazon guy will deliver your package in two days. You don't have to check in to make sure it will be delivered. You simply place your order and trust it's on its way to you.

PROTECTION
PRACTICE

If you are ever overcome with fear and feel as though you need to be protected, this is a powerful practice to protect yourself and your loved ones.

Visualize a bright light coming down from the Universe and entering through your crown chakra. Feel the light collect at your heart and burst out of your heart, forming a protective bubble around you. You can extend this bubble around others as well. Repeat: *I am safe and protected. I am loved and supported. Everything will be okay.*

My potential is
limitless.

MANIFESTING HOPE

We all have our breaking point. It's the moment that we decide we are no longer available for the things not serving our highest good, and we choose better. Manifesting hope isn't actually about hoping or wishing for better. It's making the *decision* to manifest something better. Once you make the decision, doors that you never knew existed will open. The Universe will lay out the path and guide you, but you must first make the decision to leave behind what is not serving your highest good and manifest something new.

We all have thresholds around what we will tolerate. We have thresholds around pain. We have thresholds around finances. We have thresholds around relationships. Once we dip below the line we have set for ourselves, we either fall into despair or rise up and manifest better.

I am ready to choose better.
I am the creator of my
reality and I have the power
to manifest my dreams. I am
ready to receive my desires.
So be it, so it is.

Ask For Guidance

Many times, we reach our breaking point but feel hopeless. You know you want better but have no idea how to get there. In these times, guidance is always available to you. All you have to do is ask and listen.

Find a quiet space to clear your mind and open up your journal. Ask your spirit guides or the Universe to guide you toward something better and show you the way.

Look For Signs

If you feel stuck, you can also ask for a sign. Let the Universe know what your sign is. Pick a symbol that has meaning for you but is obscure enough that you don't see it on a regular basis. This way, when you do see it, you know it's the Universe giving you a sign to let you know you're on the right track and should keep moving forward.

When I first moved to Florida, I let doubt creep in. Packing up my family and moving to a place we'd never been before was terrifying and exciting all at the same time. Was I making the right decision for my family? Would I regret it? Would we make it in this new town where we knew no one? I decided to ask for the Universe to give me a sign to let me know if I was on the right track. That sign was a rainbow. I began seeing rainbows everywhere! Every time I went for a walk or was driving, a rainbow appeared. In my house, I had two crystal lamps, and the way the sun would hit them through the window, little rainbows would reflect off the crystals onto my walls. I believe this was the Universe giving me comfort knowing I was on the right path and to keep going.

The ego tends to creep in and fill you with doubt as you get closer to stepping out of your comfort zone and into your new reality. This is when a sign can give assurance that you are on the right path.

Choose a Different Thought

When you reach a point of hopelessness and despair, it is because you have given your energy to negative thoughts and feelings. The thing about negative thoughts is they tend to breed more negative thoughts. Next thing you know, you are falling down a deep dark tunnel into a world of misery. To ask someone to simply think positive or look on the bright side is difficult.

What you can do is just start with one thought and shift it to a slightly better outcome or another way. As you begin to choose a better scenario, thought, or feeling, you can slowly begin to climb out the hole of despair and into the realm of hope.

Nourish your mind with as many good thoughts and feelings as you can. It may be as simple as feeling grateful the sun is out today or being proud of yourself for getting out of bed today. Find one thing to hold on to and allow that to blossom into hope and the possibility that more promising things are showing up in your life.

Remember, your mind is extremely powerful and you are the creator of your reality. You have the power to decide that you *are* manifesting your dreams. Once the decision is made, miracles will unfold.

If you're new to manifesting, start out small and work your way up to the big things.

MANIFESTING
MINI STEPS

When you're trying to manifest something really big, and it doesn't happen right away, it's easy to lose hope. This happens a lot with people who are brand new to the manifestation process. Their desire doesn't come to fruition right away or in the way they thought it would, and they say manifesting doesn't work.

Give yourself a small win. Maybe your big goal is to be a millionaire, but you can't even fathom what it would be like to be a millionaire. It's such a big goal compared to where you are that you don't truly believe it's possible. It can leave you feeling hopeless. If this is the case, give yourself a small win. Start with manifesting $100. Then once that happens, you try manifesting $1,000. Keep building your manifesting muscle, and your confidence and belief will follow. As you see proof of manifestation show up time and time again, your big dream of being a millionaire all of a sudden seems believable and your hope is restored.

I breathe in calmness and strength.

MANIFESTING PEACE

....

Peace is not something that comes after all wars have ended. Peace is a space within us all that can be accessed at any time. It's in the core of our being. We can hold this space for ourselves and for others. It is within this space that we manifest more peace in the world. We shine the light so others can see the way. As Mother Teresa said, "I alone cannot change the world, but I can cast a stone across the waters to create many ripples." Your energetic vibration is the stone that will cast ripples felt around the world. Let those ripples be made of peace, love, and joy.

Be the energy you wish to attract. When we witness injustices, it's easy to get angry, but by emitting feelings of anger, hate, or rage, you are giving the injustice your energy and awareness, thus giving it power. By sending out those negative feelings, you are actually drawing more of those feelings and injustices to you. So, are you supposed to just stand by and watch it happen? No. You can hold the vibration of peace and love and send it out to everyone who needs it.

Creating Space for Stillness

In order to create space for stillness, you must release what causes you to feel restless. You can unknowingly hold on to toxic energy in your body. This can come from past traumas that haven't been healed. You may be holding on to anger, resentment, bitterness, or jealousy.

Emotional Detox

We are programmed to feel shame around expressing emotions like anger, rage, or sadness. Guilt, shame, anger, and resentment can manifest in the body as tension, aches, and stiffness. One way to clear this energy is with a body scan meditation.

1. Start by sitting down with your feet planted on the ground and your back straight.
2. Begin scanning your body, starting with the top of your head all the way down to the soles of your feet.
3. Notice any tension, aches, pains, or stiffness in the body and breathe deeply into those areas.
4. With each breath, imagine creating space in those areas in between all of your cells.
5. Feel the peace wash over you as you continue this practice through-out your entire body.

I am perfect just the way I am. I am worthy of having everything I desire. My mistakes have made me stronger and helped my soul grow and evolve into the beautiful being I am.

Purge Negative Thoughts

When negative thoughts and feelings are not fully expressed, this can cause them to linger and manifest as physical stress in the body. A helpful technique for ridding yourself of these feelings is to do a journal rampage, where you write out everything that is stressing you out that you wish to release. A lot of emotions can arise from this exercise, so find a space where you feel free to openly release these emotions. Don't hold back. Let it all out. No one will see it, so allow yourself to freely express anything that comes through. This is a great time to also release any judgment or limiting beliefs that are not serving you. When you are finished, rip up the paper and throw it out or burn it, symbolizing your release of these suppressed feelings and experiences. This may become a ritual you perform once a month during the full moon as the energy of the full moon can cause many things to rise to the surface and stir up emotions.

Physical Detox

You can clear physical toxins from the body with massage, yoga, a cleanse, or a detox. Massage will help to release toxins that are in between your joints and muscles. Yoga actually helps to wring out the toxins from your organs. Detoxes and cleanses, along with drinking plenty of water, will help to remove these toxins from the body.

Declutter Your Space, Declutter Your Mind

It's hard to calm the mind and find that place of stillness when you are surrounded by clutter. A cluttered space will often lead to cluttered, overwhelmed thoughts. Just as you made space within yourself for stillness, it's now time to create space physically in your home, so you have a sacred space to relax and feel at peace. Let go of the physical objects that are taking up space and not serving a purpose, or anything that doesn't leave you feeling good. If you aren't sure whether or not to keep something, hold it in your hands and trust your feelings. Does it bring you peace, love, or joy? Is it serving a purpose in your life and contributing to your highest good? If the answer isn't immediately yes, it's time to release it. It's best to start with just one room rather than trying to tackle everything at once. Maybe even a corner of a room or a desk. Choose a space where you can retreat to when life is feeling chaotic.

Once you have decluttered, only bring things into the space that bring you love, peace, or joy. Choose things that are meaningful and make you feel good or serve a purpose. You'll be amazed at how much the practice of decluttering can impact your feelings and overall vibration, leaving you feeling renewed.

When letting go of your things, it can be helpful to feel gratitude for all the use you got out of them. Each object served its purpose. It was what you needed at the time, but now it's time to pass it on to someone else who can use it.

Give Yourself Grace

We can be our own harshest critic. It's important to remember that as human beings, we are far from perfect. Making mistakes is an integral part of our life experience, helping us to learn, grow, and evolve both here on Earth and at the soul level. Letting go of the idea of perfectionism can be one of the most freeing things you do. Accepting that there is no such thing as perfect and we are all a work in progress allows you to give yourself grace and make peace with the mistakes you've made. It breaks you free from the fear of moving forward in pursuit of your life goals.

The more fun I have,
the more abundance
I attract.

CREATIVITY AND IMAGINATION

Let's take a trip back to a time when you still allowed yourself to dream without limits. You believed in all possibilities and miracles. You didn't yet have the weight of the world sitting on your shoulders. You were free to think without limits or judgment. This was the true you, tapped into your higher self and well acquainted with the Universe.

I didn't lose my creativity or imagination. It is buried deep inside of me waiting to be discovered once again. I am ready to bring my creative and imaginative nature to the surface. I am ready to tap into my creative flow and create my reality.

Over time, the world taught you to think logically and follow the most predictable path. Chances are you were programmed to believe that creativity doesn't pay the bills and is a road that leads nowhere. This is anything but true. It is through our creativity and imagination that we open ourselves to *all* possible paths and opportunities. It is where you are led to your true purpose. It is your connection to the Universe.

Despite what you may think or what you have heard, your creativity isn't lost. It's just buried deep inside of you, and you have the power to access it whenever you are ready for it. Your imagination is still being used daily. But instead of allowing it to run free, you are simply imagining the life you think you have to live. You are imagining a predictable path that has been influenced by what society deems reasonable.

There are no limits to the mind. Your thoughts can go as far as you let them. Life can be a fun, imaginative game, or a cold, hard reality. It is up to you.

Let's say you lose your job. You can allow your mind to tell you this is the end and you're going to lose everything, or you can let your imagination get giddy with excitement at this opportunity to break free from your mediocre job and to instead start a new adventure in pursuing your passion and purpose.

Your reality is based in your thoughts. Those thoughts create feelings and those feelings affect your vibration. Your vibration determines your reality.

Creative Flow

Have you ever deeply submerged yourself into a creative project where hours went by and it felt like minutes? You were in a state of creative flow, living in the present moment. When you are living in the present moment, you activate brain-heart coherence. It's in this state that you can use the energy in your heart to impress your desires on the energetic field around you, beginning the manifestation process.

Focusing on your breathing and getting into a meditative state is a great way to get into the present moment. However, if you find yourself having difficulty with meditation, a creative outlet is another highly effective way to get into this state of creative flow and coherence.

As you immerse yourself into a creative process and tap into that flow state, you become a clear, open channel with the Universe, which allows you to receive inspired ideas and wisdom. There are so many ways to get creative, whether it's coloring, painting, knitting, cooking a new dish, or anything else that brings your attention to the creative process.

We are all creative beings and tapping into your true creative nature will awaken you to a world of possibility. You are never too old to use your imagination, dream big, and start something new.

Even trying something new like a new restaurant or taking a different route to work will help take you out of your routine and off autopilot so you can bring your awareness into the present moment.

MEDITATION
FIND YOUR SPARK

When was the last time you had a deep belly laugh? When was the last time you got lost in the moment and forgot about time? Instead of being so serious, wouldn't it be fun to let your imagination run wild? Wouldn't it feel refreshing to dream big? Wouldn't it feel good to wake up filled with joy? It's so much easier to feel good than bad. It's more fun to feel excitement than dread. Being so serious all the time can feel boring and exhausting at the same time.

It's time to find your creative spark and get in touch with that childlike imagination once again.

Here are some journal prompts to help your imagination break free and run wild:

If you knew you wouldn't be judged, what would you do? How would you be? What path would you pursue? What would you stop doing?

• • •

If you knew you couldn't fail, what would you do? How would you be? What path would you pursue?

• • •

If you had a billion dollars, what would you do today?

• • •

What is something creative you enjoyed doing as a child?

• • •

If you could build your dream day with no limits whatsoever, what would it look like?

I am worthy
of all
that I desire.

YOUR INNER CHILD

Tucked away in your heart is your inner child. Think back to when you were a young child. You were pure and innocent, not yet hardened by the world. While you cried when your basic needs demanded to be met, you were filled with love and joy. This is our natural state. It is what we are all born with. It isn't until we are programmed throughout our lives that this softness is slowly hardened, chipping away at our natural state little by little. While you have grown into an adult, your inner child is always still in there under the layers of experiences and programming that have shaped your adulthood.

Inner child healing is not just for those who have faced abuse and trauma. Everyone can benefit from healing their inner child, because we all have faced moments in our childhood that made us feel ashamed, less than, or not enough. Even moments that seemed small and insignificant, like a classmate making fun of you in second grade, or your parents making you feel ashamed for getting a bad grade on a test, have little by little chipped away at your self-worth. The experiences you consciously remember are much less numerous than what is hiding in your subconscious. While your conscious mind can't remember every single experience, your subconscious is like a library housing every memory with precise detail. The practices in this chapter will not only begin healing your inner child at the conscious level, but will also penetrate the layers of the subconscious that are holding onto these memories. As you heal your inner child, you restore your self-worth, making you an open vessel for receiving your desires.

Loving Your Inner Child

As you become reacquainted with your inner child and tap into that source of pure loving energy, you will find that manifesting becomes effortless and fun. Life becomes a game. You tap into a world of wonder where miracles happen all around you and anything is possible.

The inner child needs to be loved and nurtured, just as you would care for a newborn baby. This is how you will approach yourself from now on. When babies are learning how to eat solid foods and make a mess, you wouldn't shame them and tell them they are failures and will never learn how to eat properly. That would be absurd, right? Instead, you would offer them guidance and encourage them to keep trying. This is how you will approach yourself

INNER CHILD

MEDITATION

Dear Inner Child,

I am sorry for hiding you. I am sorry for not healing you sooner. You are safe. You are supported. You are loved. I will be here to nurture you from now on. I forgive and release all past memories that have hurt you and made you feel small. It is safe to be seen and heard. It is okay to ask and receive. With an open heart, I love and accept you unconditionally.

from now on. Don't see mistakes as failures. See them as opportunities to learn and grow, and encourage yourself to be patient and keep going.

If your children were bullied at school, you wouldn't tell them to believe the bully, and you certainly wouldn't tell them they are worthless. You would provide comfort and love. This is exactly what you need as an adult when faced with judgment and insecurities.

Even though we have grown into adults, we still need to feel loved and protected. We still need to be nurtured and reminded we are worthy. This never changes. It is true for all of humanity.

As we discussed in chapter seven, healing the past is essential in moving forward and manifesting better. Holding on to anger or resentment is only poisoning your spirit. Maybe you had a childhood where you were neglected or abused in some way. Maybe you were told you were a failure or maybe your parents didn't give you enough love or attention. It's important to know that your parents did the best they could with their level of awareness at the time. Chances are they were treated the same by their parents and it molded their parenting style. It's also important to recognize that any hurt they may have caused you was a reflection of their own pain and insecurities. Perhaps they pressured you to get a degree in something you didn't want to do. Most likely, this was about them filling a void they felt in their own life, wishing they would've taken that path.

Keep a photo of yourself as a child

to serve as a reminder of this sweet, innocent child that still lives within you and needs to be loved.

Healing Your Inner Child

It's time to dive deep and look at these past hurts so you can heal them. This isn't a fun process, but it is freeing and will help you heal your inner child. Sit and write out every experience you can think of that hurt you as a child. Think of all those moments that may seem insignificant now but slowly chipped away at your self-worth. Maybe it was the time you were grounded for getting a bad grade even though you tried your best, or the time your sibling made fun of the way you looked. All of these little moments had a part in wounding your inner child.

Talk to your inner child as though she's standing right in front of you needing the love, acceptance, and encouragement you didn't get as a child. Let her know that it is safe to be seen fully. She no longer needs to hide certain parts of herself to be accepted and loved. She no longer needs to hold on to any shameful memories because she is loved by you unconditionally. Tell her all the things you wished someone would've told you when you were little.

With your hand on your heart, go through each moment from a place of understanding and compassion. Offer forgiveness to your parents and anyone else involved, but most importantly, offer forgiveness to yourself for holding on to this moment for so long and letting it harden you. Feel your heart soften. Nurture your inner child. Let her know she is supported and loved. It is safe to release this memory and let go of the blame. It is time to move on.

Soothe Your Inner Child

Just as you would soothe a baby, soothe yourself from the aches and pains you have faced. Be gentle with yourself. Look at a photo of yourself from your childhood to visualize your inner child. You can name her and talk to her. You

can offer her the love you didn't receive as a child. As the negative self-talk begins to creep back in, look at this picture and remember to talk to yourself as you would this small child. Be kind and patient. She's still in there and needs your support more than ever.

Even if you had a charmed childhood and wonderful parents, there are still those moments where you were hurt. No one is completely immune from pain, guilt, shame, and heartache. It's powerful to heal those moments and continue to give your inner child the love and support you needed as a small child.

Life Is a Game

As we enter adulthood and the responsibilities of life pile up, it's easy to forget to have fun. You may have gone on autopilot going through the motions and forgot the importance of fun and laughter.

Children have a way of turning anything into a game and making it fun. They play and laugh and act silly. As they grow up, they are programmed to believe this behavior is immature and are even disciplined for it. The truth is that this state of play and fun is a powerful way to raise your vibration and manifest. A rule I have made for my life is the more fun I have, the more abundant I become.

Life doesn't have to be hard unless you believe it has to be. Life is a game and you make the rules. What rules do you want to make?

OVERCOMING
GUILT AND SHAME

Being open to receiving your desires is an essential part of manifesting. Just the word *desire* by itself can induce feelings of guilt and shame. This is because as a child, we felt guilt or shame around receiving. Maybe you were given a gift by a friend or family member that was expensive and you heard your parents tell them, "Oh, you shouldn't have. It's too much!" Maybe you asked for something big for your birthday and you were told it was too expensive. While these moments may seem insignificant, they were likely a pattern that caused you to develop guilt and shame around receiving your desires. Consider these questions:

Who did you have to be in order to feel loved and accepted?

• • •

What parts of you did you hide to feel accepted?

• • •

What memories leave you feeling ashamed?

Release the guilt and shame with these affirmations. Place your hand on your heart, look at yourself in the mirror and repeat:

I am worthy of love. I am worthy of abundance.

• • •

It is okay to ask for my desires. It is safe to receive my desires.

• • •

It is okay to want what I want.

I have the ability to choose new thoughts and beliefs that help me manifest a better life.

MANIFESTING YOUR FUTURE BY REVISITING YOUR PAST

As we go through life, what we observe and experience shapes our view of the world. What we observe as a young child is taken as truth no matter what. This is how generational beliefs impact us. They are beliefs that were formed from an experience an ancestor had that was observed, adopted, and passed along to future generations. For example, if your great-grandparents lived through the Great Depression and had no money and were in real danger of not being able to feed their family or have their basic needs met, they had a legitimate reason to be in a scarcity mindset. Their life was literally in jeopardy because they didn't have enough money. They learned to be fearful of losing everything and to view money as scarce. They might have viewed the rich as greedy and heartless. They had to be extremely frugal because their lives depended on it. Many of these beliefs were observed and passed on to their children.

The truth is we live in the wealthiest time ever. There is more abundance than ever before and people are getting wealthier and wealthier. Despite all the traumatizing news stories we hear, we live in the safest time ever. Thanks to technology you can start a business online for next to nothing. You can meet and collaborate with people all over the world. We live in a truly amazing time; however, generational beliefs and past memories can keep us in a fearful mindset of lack.

As a child, you may have observed your parents fighting about money. You may have been told "no," followed by, "We can't afford that" on a regular basis when asking for something you desired. You may have heard your parents say that life is hard. These situations played a role in developing your mindset and belief system.

Updating Your Beliefs

You must ask yourself if these beliefs you grew up with still hold true for you today. Just because they were true for your parents or grandparents does not mean they have to be true for you. Can you disprove them? Can you form new beliefs and look for evidence in your environment to support these upgraded beliefs? Absolutely!

By revisiting all of these scenarios, you can begin to uncover anything that is limiting your growth and expansion. By disproving these beliefs and reframing them, you can open yourself to receiving better.

Think about a storage room or closet in your home. Over the years, you keep adding stuff to this storage room that you don't need or aren't using.

Eventually, the closet will be full, leaving you with two options: clean it out or let it overflow, causing a mess. When you do finally clean it out, you wonder why you saved most of this stuff in the first place. It's served its purpose, but you no longer need it. It's just taking up space, and it's time to let it go.

This is what we do with our thoughts and beliefs. As the years go by, we continue to add more thoughts and beliefs into our subconscious closet. Eventually, if you don't clean it out, it will clutter your mind and cause a mess in your life. You need to periodically clear out the mental clutter. Go through these thoughts and beliefs and ask yourself if they are serving you. If not, it's time to let them go.

Use Your Free Will

The great thing is that we have the power of free will. We get to choose what thoughts we want to think and whether or not we want those thoughts to become dominant beliefs. Throughout life, we will always face polarizing views, but we have free will to choose what we focus on and ultimately believe. No one can take that from you.

The media is always going to tell fear-based news stories. You're bound to come across people that focus on the negative or let anger take control over them. You're going to face difficult experiences once in a while. But you get to decide if you want to give in to the negative thoughts and store them in your subconscious as negative beliefs, or if you want to choose better. You have the power to do so. You are responsible for the thoughts and beliefs you decide to hang on to. Understanding this gives you power. It doesn't allow any circumstance to take control of your life. You have the ultimate control. Once you break through the barrier of the mind and take the driver's seat, there's nothing that can hold you back from achieving your desires.

Ways to Reframe Limiting Beliefs

Overcoming limiting beliefs is not a one and done effort. Limiting beliefs will continue to arise throughout your life. The belief that you hold dominant in your subconscious will prevail. By continuing to disprove limiting beliefs and by replacing them with something better, you can rewire your subconscious. Your subconscious learns through repetition, so if it hears something enough times, it will begin to believe it and look for evidence in your environment to support it. Try these methods to begin that process of rewiring.

Journaling

Writing is powerful because it channels energy through your heart chakra down your arm and into your hand. It also uses a different neural pathway than is used when typing. Here is what my journaling process looks like:

1. Write out your desires, and as you go through each one, bring awareness to any thoughts that immediately come up to say you can't have what you desire. (Desire: *I am a millionaire.* Limiting belief: *I'm not good with money and wouldn't know how to be responsible with that much money.*)

2. Simply observe this limiting belief and ask if it's true. (*Could I learn to be responsible with money? Of course!*)

3. Disprove this limiting belief and reframe it. (*More money means more resources. I can afford to hire a financial advisor to teach me everything I need to know about being responsible with money; therefore, it is safe and possible for me to be a millionaire.*)

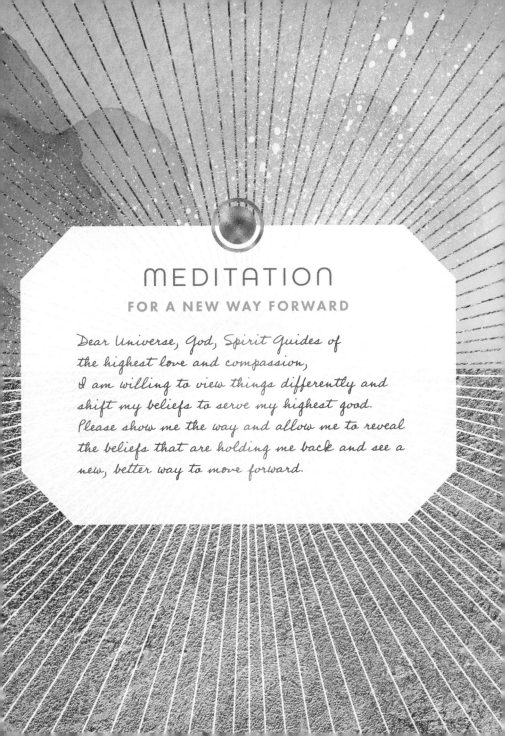

MEDITATION

FOR A NEW WAY FORWARD

Dear Universe, God, Spirit Guides of
the highest love and compassion,
I am willing to view things differently and
shift my beliefs to serve my highest good.
Please show me the way and allow me to reveal
the beliefs that are holding me back and see a
new, better way to move forward.

Here are some more examples of common limiting beliefs that may be holding you back and how you can reframe them and tell a new story:

* ✳ *I'm too old.* ›››› *I have so much knowledge and experience to share.*
* ✳ *I'm too young.* ›››› *I have plenty of time to learn.*
* ✳ *I'm not smart enough.* ›››› *I am resourceful and can figure it out.*
* ✳ *Making money is hard.* ›››› *When I do what I love, abundance will always follow.*
* ✳ *Wealthy people are greedy and dishonest.* ›››› *I am a good person. The amount in my bank account will not change that. Good people do good things with money. The world needs more good people with money.*
* ✳ *I'll never find true love.* ›››› *I love myself unconditionally; therefore, I am a magnet for attracting someone who will love me unconditionally.*
* ✳ *It's always something.* ›››› *I am always supported and things always work out in my favor.*

How does that shift in belief feel? At first, you will probably feel resistance to this. You may even be rolling your eyes. This is normal. It is your subconscious working really hard to keep you safe in the status quo. It thinks your current beliefs are the ultimate truth, so it will resist contradicting beliefs. Not to worry. You can retrain your subconscious to shift to new, empowering beliefs. This is done through repetition.

Recording affirmations yourself works well because your subconscious will recognize your voice and be less likely to doubt it.

Affirmations and Hypnosis

The subconscious learns through repetition, which is why
affirmations are so effective in rewiring limiting beliefs.
Speaking affirmations out loud, writing them down,
and reading them repeatedly is a great way to ensure
your subconscious is being rewired for your new,
empowering beliefs.

A trick I learned is to record my affirmations in an
audio file on my phone and listen to them often. Listening to
affirmations is especially helpful when you're falling asleep
because that is when the subconscious is the most vulnerable.

Anchoring

You can use your happiest past memories to help you manifest more positive
things in the future. One way to do this is with anchoring. You can anchor good,
high-vibrational feelings with a scent or music. This way, whenever you smell
that scent or listen to that music, you can instantly bring yourself into a high-
vibrational state, allowing you to align with the frequency you want to manifest.

Have you ever heard a song that instantly brings you back in time to a
good memory? You feel all the feelings you felt at the time and it's like you are
living the experience all over again.

I remember my first job out of college was at a call center, and it was by
far the worst job I've ever had. I dreaded waking up every morning and going
to this place. There were no windows, we were given a half hour lunch break
and literally had a boss standing over our shoulder every minute of every day
grading us.

I will never forget boldly walking through the doors one morning and placing my headphones on my boss's desk telling him I found a new job. I walked out of there and got in my car. "I Can See Clearly Now" started playing on the radio, and I just remember smiling so big and feeling this huge weight completely melt off my shoulders. I was so relieved to close that chapter and excited about what the future had in store for me.

Now every time I hear that song, I am instantly brought back into that moment of pure bliss and a huge smile crosses my face. It's now my go-to, feel-good, high-vibe song. Whenever I'm feeling down or whenever I want to get in a high-vibe state and manifest my desires, I'll listen to it over and over again while visualizing what I want.

This is what anchoring is. You are anchoring a powerful memory associated with a high-vibrational feeling. By pairing this with a song or scent, you can instantly be taken to that high-vibrational feeling whenever you want to manifest.

You can also anchor with a scent. For me, the smell of fresh-cut grass instantly brings back happy memories of summer break as a child. The smell of Christmas trees brings me right back to the excitement of Christmas.

Alternatively, you may also have negative anchors. For example, thinking about a spider might cause you to feel anxious or a particular song may bring back a painful or negative memory.

ANCHORING
WITH SCENTS AND MUSIC

I am going to walk you through how to pair a new scent or song with a high-vibrational state. After doing so, the song or scent will serve as a trigger to instantly put you in a high-vibrational state.

Recall a strong, beneficial emotional state. See what you saw, feel what you felt, hear what you heard. Relive the experience in your mind.

Pick an anchor: this can be smelling a scent, listening to a song, or even pressing your thumb and middle finger together. Once you are in that high-vibrational state, use the anchor and hold those feelings with the anchor for a few seconds.

Break the state by engaging your brain. Do a math equation, ask yourself a strange question or do something else to break you out of the high-vibe state.

Then go back to step one and repeat the steps multiple times.

After repeating five or more times, test this out by using the anchor to see if it triggers that high-vibrational state. If it does, you have established a strong anchor that you can now use anytime to get yourself instantly in a high-vibrational state. If it doesn't trigger a high-vibrational state, then keep repeating the steps until a strong connection has been established.

I am consciously
creating my future.

18

LUCID DREAMING

Is there a shortcut to manifesting? We know that acting as if you've already manifested what you want will help you align with that reality and make the quantum shift. Lucid dreaming, when you are aware that you are in a dream, is a shortcut to making this quantum shift. Imagine being able to do something you've always wanted to but were too afraid to try. Your fears, limiting beliefs, and lack of self-confidence might hold you back in the real world, but if you knew you were in a dream, you could pursue anything you want fearlessly. You could practice being this next-level version of yourself who is confident and fearless.

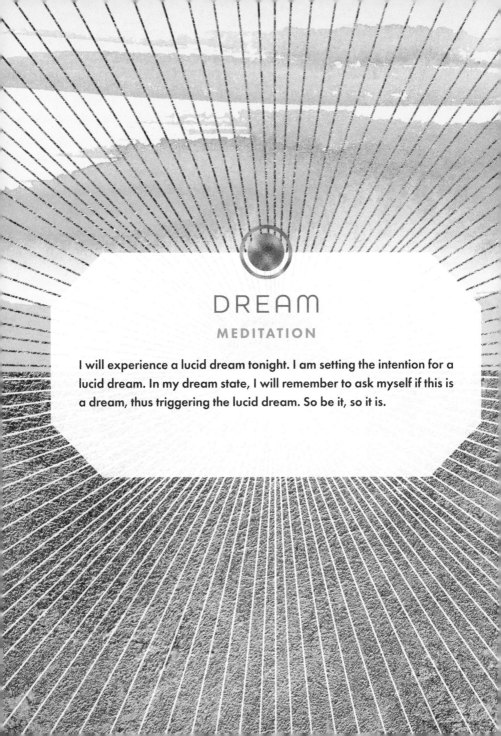

DREAM
MEDITATION

I will experience a lucid dream tonight. I am setting the intention for a lucid dream. In my dream state, I will remember to ask myself if this is a dream, thus triggering the lucid dream. So be it, so it is.

Research has shown that you can rewire your brain in a lucid dreaming state. Studies have been done with athletes who have used lucid dreaming to practice their skills and increase their athletic ability, and the results were nothing short of miraculous. They did in fact increase their athletic ability even though they were not practicing their skills in the physical world.

You can use lucid dreams to practice anything, even your ideal reality. The thing about visualizing your goals while awake is that our subconscious still dominates the mind the majority of the time. So even if you are consciously focused on your desires, limiting beliefs and self-conscious thoughts can linger and hold you back. In the dream world, your subconscious is more vulnerable to being rewired. This is why affirmations are far more powerful in a lucid dream state.

Create New Pathways

Your brain can create new neural pathways in this lucid dream state. Imagine taking the same route to work every single day. At first, you're learning the new route, so you're aware and focused. After a while, it becomes default. You don't have to think about it or use your GPS. You've built a strong pathway and it becomes second nature. Now, if you changed your route and went a new way, the same process would happen. At first, you'd have to focus and be

consciously aware of where you're going. But after a while, you develop a new neural pathway, and it becomes your new default.

Lucid dreaming allows you to take these new routes without actually taking them in real life. By living out your desires in a lucid dream state, you will be creating new neural pathways that will rewire your brain and the limiting beliefs associated with manifesting your desires.

Lucid dreams are where quantum shifts can happen. It's as though you are stepping into a new reality. This can be a place where you practice your dream reality and try things that would normally make you self-conscious or fill you with doubt.

Lucid Dreams as Visualization

Visualization is so powerful in the manifestation process. What better way to visualize your dreams than by stepping into them via a lucid dream? The Universe doesn't differentiate between reality and fantasy. The Universe responds to your thoughts, feelings, and vibration, so even though you're dreaming, the Universe is viewing this as reality and aligning you with the right opportunities to support this new reality.

It's also thought that you can connect to your higher self in a lucid dream. Who do you want to be? A published author? A celebrity? A millionaire? You can step into this persona in this state, preparing yourself for the new reality you wish to create.

Keep a dream journal next to your bed and write in it as soon as you wake up while everything is still fresh in your mind.

LEARN

LUCID DREAMING

Follow these steps to get into a lucid dreaming state:

*Keep a dream journal. Be as detailed as possible
and note anything strange that would be a giveaway
that you were in a dream. Notice any patterns you
see over time that indicate you're dreaming.*

*Throughout the day, stop and ask yourself, "Am I
dreaming?" Do this at different times throughout the
day. You will build the habit and by doing that, you will
find yourself asking this question within your dreams.
You can then look for anything strange from step
one that would be a giveaway that it's a dream.*

*Before you fall asleep, you can set the intention to
lucid dream. As you are falling asleep, tell yourself
repeatedly that you will have a lucid dream. As you
fall asleep your brain is in the theta state, which
is a hypnotic state and is highly suggestable.*

If I can see it
in my mind and believe
it in my heart,
I can manifest it into
my reality.

CHAPTER

19

CREATING A VISION BOARD

Visualization is a key component of the Law of Attraction, yet it's the one that people tend to struggle with the most. This is because the brain has trouble holding a static image. This is why you may be trying to hold a vision in your mind and find that every few seconds, your mind begins to wander. Try to visualize your dream car. You probably have an idea of the make, model, and color, but you're probably not seeing the details clearly unless you're actually looking at the car or a picture of the car. Vision boards are a tool that can help you get clear on what you desire and solidify an image in your mind's eye.

This book is a manifestation of my 2018 vision board. In 2020, I was doing a vision board workshop and showed some of my old vision boards to the class. My 2018 vision board was filled with images, affirmations, and words about being a published author. I had long forgotten about that board. Somewhere along the way, I listened to some other authors tell me how impossible it was to get a book deal. They explained how you have to write a proposal, get an agent, and pitch it to dozens of publishers only to deal with getting rejected over and over again. I let them plant the seed of doubt and forgot all about becoming an author. But during that vision board workshop, I looked at this board and remembered the excitement I felt around it. I felt called to it. I began opening myself up to the possibility of it once again and renewed my vision and excitement. Two months later, I was contacted by a publisher about writing this book. I have no doubt that revisiting my old vision board is what set this in motion.

Have you ever talked about something or searched for something online, and the next thing you know, you start seeing ads for it on social media? Just like the targeted ads on social media, the Universe will present opportunities targeted to you based on what you focus on. When you get aligned with what you want, the Universe will start custom-tailoring your opportunities to match what you want. When you put something on your vision board, you are telling your subconscious this is important, so when opportunities in your environment appear, your conscious mind will process them.

How to Make Your Vision Board

There are many different ways to create a vision board. You can use a cork board, create a digital board, or even use a notebook. Your vision board can include photos, words, quotes, and affirmations. Its purpose is to help you get clear on your grand vision and bring it to life with visuals.

With this vision board, I bring my desires to life and give gratitude for them as though they have already manifested. I have unwavering faith they will be delivered to me in divine timing. It is done!

I have a physical board where I put words, affirmations, and inspiring quotes. You want to put it in a place where you see it daily. I keep mine in my closet, so it's the first thing I see every morning when I am getting dressed. I also have a digital vision board on Pinterest where I find images that represent my vision. Pinterest is a great tool because it's a search engine that allows you to find specific images and organize them on digital boards. You can even create multiple digital vision boards for each area of your life— purpose, career, relationships, health, travel, hobbies, and so on.

As I'm searching through the photos on Pinterest and adding them to my board, I treat it as though I'm searching through the catalog of life and placing my order with the Universe. All I need to do is place my order, then trust that it will be delivered. I don't need to worry about it or obsess over it. I have unwavering faith that the Universe will find the best path to deliver my desires in divine timing.

When I was living in Illinois, it was my dream to move to Florida one day. I created a Pinterest board called My Beach Retreat and kept adding photos of everything I would want in my dream home in Florida. Even though I didn't know if I'd ever get the chance to move there, I created this board and began planning out how I wanted to design my home, room by room. I accumulated all sorts of pictures of everything from kitchen cabinets to furniture and accessories. Every time I looked at that board, I would imagine myself in that house and swell up with joy and excitement. I would imagine the warm sun on my skin, the smell of the beach, and the feeling of absolute peace and serenity living in my happy place. I now live in that dream home. I once put a photo of each room in my house next to the photos on that vision board, and they are almost identical! Except the real thing is even better. That's the thing about the Universe. When you trust that your desires will be delivered, they end up being even better than you imagined.

Goal Setting

We gradually grow over time. Try to choose goals you can wrap your mind around. For example, I can wrap my mind around $1 million; however, I can't even fathom making a billion dollars. It's so beyond what my mind can conceive, I know I'd be filled with doubt. Everyone has their threshold of what they deem conceivable. Challenge yourself to push just beyond that, but don't overdo it to the point where you get filled with doubt, fear, and frustration.

You can take a photo of your vision board and save it as your lock screen on your phone or as a screensaver on your computer.

The whole purpose of this is to get clear on your goals and have fun! This shouldn't feel like a chore. If you start to feel overwhelmed or stressed, walk away and come back to it when you're in a better state of mind.

Vision boards help the subconscious accept your new reality by seeing it repeatedly. It allows the Reticular Activating System to develop a connection between you and your desires and tag them as important, so when opportunities show up in your environment, you become consciously aware of them. Remember, the subconscious learns through repetition, so placing the vision board where you can see the images often will help the subconscious become familiarized with what you want.

Looking at your vision board should feel good. It should excite you and open you up to a world of possibilities. If you find that it is giving you doubt or you are looking at it from a place of desperation, then examine the beliefs that are coming up for you.

Do you feel like you must have these things to be happy? If so, revisit some of the practices that focus on internal work presented in the previous chapters.

Do you feel like your board isn't realistic or like you can't have these things? Do you feel unworthy of these things? Once again, revisit the previous chapters and bring awareness to the beliefs that are limiting you. Remember, the only limitations are the ones your mind creates.

Vision boards are not a requirement for manifestation. Just like all the other tools throughout this book, they are meant to help you. If you feel resistance or don't need one to create a crystal-clear vision in your mind, then don't make one. Some people prefer writing out their desires in a journal or using meditation to visualize. The method doesn't matter. What matters is that you hold a clear vision and have unwavering faith it will manifest in your reality. Let go and trust the Universe.

VISUALIZE
YOUR DREAM DAY

Look at your entire life as a whole, and visualize what your dream day looks like. Consider:

*If you had all the money in the world,
what would your day look like?*

• • •

Who would be with you? Where would you live?

• • •

*What would you do for fun?
What would be your purpose?*

All these areas of your life are interconnected and all affect one another. Try to see the big picture—the grand vision.

Joy, love,
and abundance are my
natural state.

MANIFESTING MORE HAPPINESS

Happiness is found within. No external circumstance is going to make you happy. To prove this, just look at all the people with every advantage and resource who are miserable and all the people living under dire circumstances who are blissful.

We are programmed with this notion that happiness comes from some external milestone. The problem with this thought process is the bar is continually raised, leaving us unfulfilled and constantly wanting more. We keep telling ourselves that once we hit that next milestone, we will be happy, but the happiness continues to elude us.

We have it all backwards. It's the happiness that comes first, followed by success. When we focus on the positive, we attract positive opportunities through the Law of Attraction that help us manifest our version of success and fulfillment in life.

A rule I have made for my life is to do more of what I love and less of what drains my energy. In doing so, I manifest more things that I love while the things that drain me show up less and less in my reality. For years, I worked so hard to achieve success and happiness. What it left me with was anything but the happiness I was yearning for. Instead, I was experiencing stress and anxiety that manifested into panic attacks and burnout. It was when I let go and quit trying to force it that I was finally able to lead a life of fulfillment. When I put my happiness first, I raised my vibration, and every opportunity I dreamed of presented itself effortlessly.

You will continually improve your life. I see a lot of people stress over what they want to manifest. There's no need to stress. Whatever you don't manifest now, you can manifest in the future. This is not a one-time thing. This isn't a genie that only grants you three wishes. You can use the tools in this book to manifest anything you desire throughout your lifetime. You can and will continue to create a grander version of your life. As you step into your higher self, you will feel worthy and capable of so much more. This is just the beginning.

Manifesting Abundance

The subconscious will not contradict itself, so if it believes in lack, it can't also believe in abundance. This is why it's crucial to stop talking in terms of debt and start affirming how much money you desire.

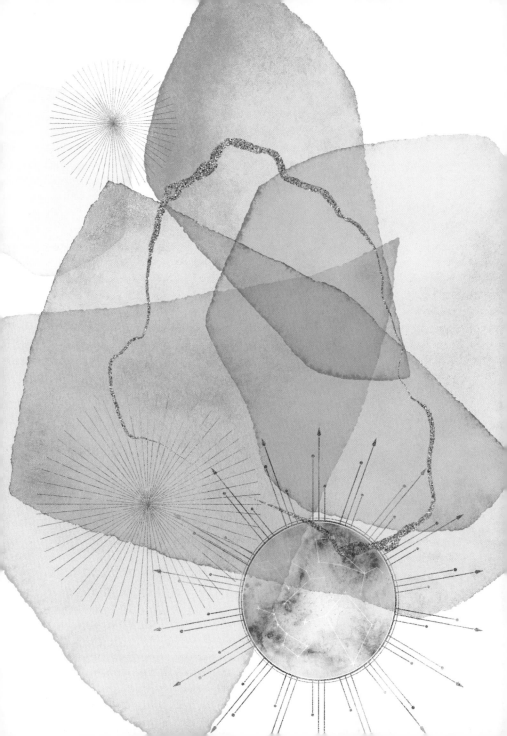

The job of the subconscious is to protect you. If you believe money is the root of all evil, your subconscious will make sure you stay in debt to protect you. A way to reframe this common belief that has been embedded in our society is to remember that it's not money that is evil. It is the person holding the money that is giving off bad or good energy. Are you a good person? Would that change if you became wealthy tomorrow? Of course not! You would still be you. All of these beliefs we've been fed that say rich people are bad or greedy are simply not true. You can find poor people who are greedy and you can also find rich people who are generous. It goes back to the person holding the money and the energy they are putting out.

Once you can disprove and reframe these common limiting beliefs around money and becoming wealthy, you can open the flood-gates to abundance in your life. Abundance is your natural state. There is more than enough to go around. Think of how much would be possible if everyone tapped into the power of abundance and let go of the idea of lack.

To become more abundant, start feeling love and gratitude for what you already have—no matter how little. Give gratitude for your paycheck, even if it's not as much as you'd like to make. Be grateful for all the money you've received throughout your life.

Think of one thing you can add to your life

that would bring you joy, and think of one thing you can subtract from your life that drains you.

Giving from a place of love sends a strong signal to the Universe that you are ready to receive. I made up a rule in my life that every time I release money from a place of love, it will always be replenished. It has held true for years. I receive money in so many unexpected ways and it's almost always more than what I spent.

You get to choose the rules and mantras for your life. I choose to affirm things that feel good and support the life I want to live.

Manifesting Love

One of the most common questions I get is how to manifest love. Oftentimes, the question is posed as, "How do I make my love interest fall in love with me?" First of all, you can't make anyone do anything. Everyone has free will to choose. You cannot force someone to think or act in a way that goes against their free will, and the more you force something, the more you repel it.

What you can do is attract someone who will love you. The way you do that is through self-love. Remember, what you put out is what you attract back to you. How can you expect anyone to fall in love with you if you don't even love yourself? If your thoughts, feelings, and vibration are aligned with self-love, you will become a magnet for more love. This is why confidence is sexy. The opposite is also true. The more critical you are of yourself, the more you will attract that type of energy from people.

Maybe you want to reconnect with your spouse and revive your relationship. Most people will try to do this by changing the other person. This is only setting you up for disappointment. You cannot change someone else. The only thing you can change and control is yourself. Remember, the energy you are putting into the relationship is the energy you will attract back. We tend to put high expectations on the other person, but rarely look at ourselves to see if we are meeting those same expectations. Instead of putting the expectations on your partner, put them on yourself and watch your partner follow your lead.

Do you want your partner to spend more time with you? Start giving your partner your undivided attention. Do you want to go on a romantic getaway? Plan the first trip. Do you yearn for more affection or physical attention? Be the one to start giving that to your partner.

Manifesting Health

We have all been taught to believe that our genes, as well as our environment, are responsible for many of our health problems. It's true that our genes may give us a predisposition for things like cancer and blood disorders, but your cells have the ability to turn your genes on or off. Your cells are always listening and taking direction from your mind. This is the mind-body connection. Eastern medicine has always known this. Western medicine is now acknowledging that this connection does in fact exist because neurotransmitters are located throughout the entire body and touch every single cell.

Thank you, Universe,
for guiding me back to my
internal default state
of happiness. I have the ability
to tap into this state
whenever I need to and can
let go of the idea that
my happiness is controlled by
external circumstances.
I move forward with love,
gratitude, and zest
for life.

What has been discovered with epigenetics is that our thoughts and feelings can turn genes on or off. For example, if cancer runs in your family, you may be worried that you will get cancer. These thoughts and feelings that focus on the very thing you don't want may actually be turning those cancer genes on. It goes even further. Your thoughts and feelings are also giving your cells direction on what should manifest in the body.

This is why stress leads to disease. It is sending the message that there is "dis-ease" in your body, so that is what manifests. Think about all of the subliminal messaging we are constantly encountering about our bodies, whether it's the beauty company telling us our skin has wrinkles or the pharmaceutical company telling us the latest drug we need to treat ailments. Furthermore, when you ask someone what they think of their health or body, many times you will hear a list of problems that all give a negative impression of how they look and feel. *I need to lose weight. I look so old. I have chronic back pain. I am in a constant brain fog. These headaches won't go away.* All of this language continually affirms that those things will remain a constant in their life.

The good news is you can start sending positive directions to your cells by focusing on feeling youthful, vibrant, and energetic. Give gratitude for your magnificent body. Your cells are working around the clock to keep you well. Your heart is beating all the time to keep you alive. Your brain, heart, and gut are working every second to ensure your body is running smoothly. Your eyes allow you to see the beauty in this world. Your taste buds allow you to enjoy eating. Your legs have enabled you to walk, run, and play. When you get a cut, bruise, or cold, your body repairs itself. In this lifetime, we get this one body. When we lose our health, other things like money or the perfect job don't seem to matter as much. Give gratitude every day for the amazing body that has taken you through life and will continue to work hard for you every second of every day.

You Can't Mess This Up

You can't mess this up. Life is a game. The goal is not perfection. The goal is to continually learn, grow, and experience what you are meant to in this lifetime. You are human. You will make mistakes. Sometimes those mistakes will be the result of letting your ego guide you instead of your higher self. Other times, those mistakes are actually blessings in disguise. It could very well be the Universe throwing a wrench in your plan to steer you toward a better path. You will still think negative thoughts and listen to your ego instead of your higher self at times.

When you find yourself in these situations where past limiting beliefs are holding you back or you fall back into a negative mindset, give yourself grace and allow yourself time to integrate the processes discussed in this book. This is not a one and done. It is a lifelong journey of learning and growing. You can refer back to the various subjects in this book as situations arise, but keep in mind that no matter what comes up in your external environment, you always have control. It is within you that you create your reality, and that is where you will always find the answers you're seeking.

It's important to trust your feelings, intuition, higher self, and most of all, the Universe. You have the wisdom of the entire Universe within you. You can tap into it whenever you need to. Never forget how powerful you truly are.

HEALING
MEDITATION

This is a practice I love to do when I am not feeling well or have pain in my body.

1

Rate your pain on a scale of 1 to 10.

2

Visualize a golden, shimmering light coming down through your head and flowing to the area in pain.

3

Breathe into this area of the body and visualize little bits of shimmering light healing and repairing every cell perfectly.

4

Rate your pain again on the same scale after this practice to see how much you have improved.

RESOURCES

FROM THE LAW OF ATTRACTION TRIBE

Subliminal Audio Meditations and Affirmations

• • •

Law of Attraction Tribe Podcast

• • •

Law of Attraction 5-Day Course

• • •

Free resource library:
thelawofattractiontribe.com/free-resources

• • •

Browse my vision board printables,
manifestation bundles, and additional resources at
thelawofattractiontribe.com/shop.

RECOMMENDED READING

THE SECRET
by Rhonda Byrne

• • •

THE POWER
by Rhonda Byrne

• • •

THE MAGIC
by Rhonda Byrne

• • •

THE SCIENCE OF GETTING RICH
by Wallace Wattles

• • •

*RICH AS F*CK*
by Amanda Frances

• • •

YOU ARE A BADASS AT MAKING MONEY
by Jen Sincero

• • •

THE POWER OF YOUR SUBCONSCIOUS MIND
by Joseph Murphy

• • •

LAW OF ATTRACTION TRIBE WORKBOOK
by Stephanie Keith

ESSENTIAL AFFIRMATIONS

* I am filled with happiness and gratitude.
* I choose to be happy right now.
* I am filled with joy.
* I am consciously creating my future.
* I am happy, healthy, and whole.
* I am in a high-vibrational state.
* My possibilities are endless.
* Everything always works out for me.
* I will act with intention today.
* My actions create constant prosperity.
* There is a continuous flow of money into my life.
* I am aligned with the energy of abundance.
* I attract wealth and abundance with every breath I take.
* I am worthy of receiving money.
* I make money doing what I love.
* My financial future is secure.
* I attract success and prosperity.
* I attract money through love and joy.
* I manifest my dreams effortlessly.
* It's easy for me to achieve my goals.
* My life is abundant and full of opportunity.
* I have the power to create my life.
* My thoughts become things.

* All is well in my world.
* My energy creates my reality.
* I attract my desires with ease.
* I don't have to be perfect. I just need to be me.
* I am capable of dealing with any problems I face.
* All I need is within me.
* I am exactly where I need to be right now.
* I am positive and at ease.
* I am healthy and strong.
* I love my body.
* I am filled with wellness and vitality.
* I am a magnet for good health.
* My cells are renewing my health every day.
* I have healing energy flowing through my body.
* Every cell in my body is filled with light.
* I am thankful for my radiant health.
* I feel renewed and re-energized.
* Miracles happen in my life all the time.
* What I focus on is attracted into my life.
* I am divinely guided toward my destiny.
* Divine opportunities gravitate into my life.
* The answers I need are already within me.
* The Universe is responding to my thoughts and feelings.

ACKNOWLEDGMENTS

To my amazing mom, thank you for always supporting me and my crazy ideas. You introduced me to the Law of Attraction, which took me down this incredible, fulfilling path, and I am forever grateful.

To my dad, thank you for always encouraging me to dream big and make waves.

I want to thank Rage Kindelsperger for offering me this opportunity to manifest my lifelong dream of writing a book and leaving my mark on the world.

Thank you to my editor Katie Moore and the amazing team at Quarto Publishing for helping me bring my vision to life.

To my husband Dustin, your support means the world to me. Thank you for encouraging me to follow my dreams. I love you.

To my children, Alexis, Amelia, and Aidyn, thank you for inspiring me every day. You are my whole world and I love you more than words could ever express.

I want to thank my loyal friends who have cheered me on through this whole process and my tribe, which is filled with beautiful souls who have supported me along my wild journey.

And most of all, I want to thank you, the reader. None of this would be possible without you.

ABOUT THE AUTHOR

Stephanie Keith is an author, the founder and CEO of Law of Attraction Tribe LLC, and host of the Law of Attraction Tribe Podcast. After more than a decade in the corporate world, Stephanie broke free from the 9 to 5 grind to create a life filled with freedom and abundance. She now empowers others to do the same. Her passion is teaching women how to reprogram societal conditioning and trust their intuition to guide them down their most fulfilling path. Stephanie lives in Tampa, Florida, with her husband and three kids.

You can connect with Stephanie on Instagram @lawofattractiontribe and find out more at thelawofattractiontribe.com.

© 2022 by Quarto Publishing Group USA Inc.
Text © 2022 by Stephanie Keith

First published in 2022 by Rock Point, an imprint of The Quarto Group,
142 West 36th Street, 4th Floor, New York, NY 10018, USA
T (212) 779-4972 F (212) 779-6058 www.Quarto.com

All rights reserved. No part of this book may be reproduced in any form without written permission of the copyright owners. All images in this book have been reproduced with the knowledge and prior consent of the artists concerned, and no responsibility is accepted by producer, publisher, or printer for any infringement of copyright or otherwise, arising from the contents of this publication. Every effort has been made to ensure that credits accurately comply with information supplied. We apologize for any inaccuracies that may have occurred and will resolve inaccurate or missing information in a subsequent reprinting of the book.

Rock Point titles are also available at discount for retail, wholesale, promotional, and bulk purchase. For details, contact the Special Sales Manager by email at specialsales@quarto.com or by mail at The Quarto Group, Attn: Special Sales Manager, 100 Cummings Center Suite 265D, Beverly, MA 01915 USA.

10 9 8 7 6 5 4 3 2 1

ISBN: 978-1-63106-974-1

Publisher: Rage Kindelsperger
Creative Director: Laura Drew
Managing Editor: Cara Donaldson
Senior Editor: Katharine Moore
Cover and Interior Design: Chika Azuma

Printed in China

This book provides general information on various widely known and widely accepted methods for improving happiness and confidence. However, it should not be relied upon as recommending or promoting any specific diagnosis or method of treatment for a particular condition, and it is not intended as a substitute for medical advice or for direct diagnosis and treatment of a medical condition by a qualified physician. Readers who have questions about a particular condition, possible treatments for that condition, or possible reactions from the condition or its treatment should consult a physician or other qualified healthcare professional.